Achieving Successful
Organizational Transformation

Achieving Successful
Organizational Transformation

*David A. Whitsett
and Irving R. Burling*

QUORUM BOOKS
Westport, Connecticut • London

Library of Congress Cataloging-in-Publication Data

Whitsett, David A.
  Achieving successful organizational transformation / David A.
Whitsett and Irving R. Burling.
    p.   cm.
  Includes bibliographical references and index.
  ISBN 1–56720–026–5 (alk. paper)
    1. Organizational change—United States—Case studies.
  2. Financial services industry—United States—Case studies.
  I. Burling, Irving R.   II. Title.
  HD58.8.W493   1996
  658.4′06—dc20   95–23708

British Library Cataloguing in Publication Data is available.

Library of Congress Catalog Card Number: 95–23708
ISBN: 1–56720–026–5

First published in 1996

Quorum Books, 88 Post Road West, Westport, CT 06881
An imprint of Greenwood Publishing Group, Inc.

Printed in the United States of America

The paper used in this book complies with the
Permanent Paper Standard issued by the National
Information Standards Organization (Z39.48–1984).

10 9 8 7 6 5 4 3 2 1

To my wife Pearl, who has given so much to me, to our children, to our company, and to the accomplishment described in this book.

To my daughters Lisa and Laurel, who are the most important people in my world, who inspire all I accomplish, and who are helping me to grow.

Contents

Acknowledgments

We have had a great deal of help with this book. Most importantly, we received the gracious cooperation of the boards of directors and executives of the two companies involved. They agreed to allow this story to be told and without that permission, this book would not exist.

Second, we want to offer our profound gratitude to the many members of the companies who gave so much of their time and of themselves during the hours of interviewing required to piece together this account. The story is theirs and many of them gave freely of their files, their recollections, and their feelings to help it be told. Special thanks to Tom Olson, John Waggoner, Kevin Lentz and Dan Meylink who read and critiqued drafts and helped us improve the book. Any inaccuracies are, of course, our responsibility and not theirs and it should be noted that this book is based primarily on the view of just one of the companies' presidents and, as such, may not be a balanced representation.

Fran Athington, the secretary in the University of Northern Iowa department of psychology, demonstrated her extraordinary good humor and patience by helping us through what must have seemed to be endless revisions of the manuscript. Thank you, Fran.

Irv Burling especially wants to thank his friends Keith Frost and John Olson, as well as his three children Kris, Dan, and Dave for their faith in him and the encouragement he needed to undertake writing this book.

Finally, to the people at the Greenwood Publishing Group, especially our editors Marcy Weiner, Elisabetta Linton, and Norine Mudrick we offer our thanks for their patience, their help and their belief in the value of our project.

1

An Overview

INTRODUCTION

This is the story of what may be the most unusual combination of two companies in the history of American business. In 1990, a permanent affiliation between CUNA Mutual Insurance Society, headquartered in Madison, Wisconsin, and Century Companies of America, with its home office in Waverly, Iowa became a reality. It is important to note at the outset the phrase, "a permanent affiliation," because it describes a relationship unlike any other of which we are aware. This is much more than a joint venture, much more than a strategic alliance, but it is not a merger; it is not an acquisition of one company by another; therefore the phrase, "a permanent affiliation," is most assuredly not simply a euphemism. It describes how two companies faced the challenges that threaten the financial services industry of America at its most fundamental level.

The affiliation was the result of the vision and untiring efforts of two creative, energetic and dedicated chief executive officers (CEOs) and the creative energy of the companies' staffs and boards of directors. The affiliation had its beginning in November of 1986 when the two CEOs happened to meet at an executive seminar at Harvard University. At that meeting they first discussed together their views of the challenges facing their industry and the inadequacies of the conventional solutions that were being tried by other organizations. Over the ensuing three and one-half years they guided their respective companies along a path that resulted in a relationship that allows the companies to meet the challenges they had agreed existed and to do so while protecting, and, in fact, enhancing the interests of their respective constituencies.

This was not easily accomplished. Many obstacles had to be overcome, and significant work still needs to be done to maximize the potential synergies of the affiliated companies. But, through it all, the vision of what could be has sustained the participants, and it is apparent that the vision is within reach. There are myriad technical details involved when companies seek to affiliate, and we will explain them here to make our story understandable, but our primary purpose is to tell the human side of this story. People's lives are changed when companies combine, no matter what form that combination takes. It requires tremendous courage, energy, and commitment from many people to do what has been, and continues to be, done here, and this is the story of those people and how this undertaking has affected them. In Chapter 4 we will discuss the trouble that the industry was experiencing, but in spite of those tough times the affiliation during the past five years has produced some amazing results in its individual life business. Note the following:

- The sales force for individual sales has more than doubled while the cost of distribution per unit (for established Plan America units) is gradually decreasing
- The integration of blocks of business into communities of interest, described in later chapters, will in the long term generate nearly $20 million in productivity savings. Productivity savings means that the entire block of individual business will cost that much less to administer than before the affiliation.
- While product mix has changed, it is worth noting that assets have increased by more than 50 percent.
- Integration of some functions, namely investments, legal and information systems, has saved well over $1 million a year.
- While many insurance companies are continuing to down size their organizations, the affiliation has added additional distribution channels and the staff to administer the individual block of business has increased over three fold.
- Before the affiliation, Century processed approximately 30,000 applications through their single distribution system each year. Additional distribution systems have been added in the affiliation process so that Century is now processing over 1 million applications each year.

It is also important to note that these achievements have taken place under difficult conditions in the insurance industry. These conditions, discussed further in Chapter 4, have continued to plague the industry to the present time. Some illustrations follow:

Shannon (1993), who is CEO of the Fidelity Union Insurance Company, commented on some of the trends shaping the insurance industry today.

- As some companies seek a sustainable future, they will sponsor multiple distribution systems and only some will include the traditional career agency system.
- Thee margins on products widely sold today, asset accumulation products, are too thin to support the traditional career system.
- As companies continue to build sustainable futures, especially the medium and small companies, you can expect more mergers.

Cass (1993) points out that total premiums are growing but at a rate approaching inflation and obviously expenses cannot continue to grow at the same rate without having a negative impact on unit costs.

Stein (1994), in answering the question, Is the (insurance) industry out of the doldrums at last?, offers the following observations:

- Small companies are spending, on average, about 28 percent more of their premium to acquire new business than are the large companies.

- The industry continues to be sluggish in the growth of sales and premiums.
- Annuity accumulation products, which have thin margins will continue to hold back earnings growth.
- Products with thin margins will continue to put a strain on companies as they attempt to compete with other providers who have superior service in asset accumulation products because of the number of years that they been offering these products.
- Niche players are apt to become more visible and successful in the market.
- Companies who do not have control of their distribution channels, or who are not successful in cutting more expense out of their marketing or administrative costs will continue to struggle in the marketplace.
- Improvement of industry results will only happen after there is a change in the operations and the consolidation of companies that are unable to make the transition.

The message continues to be clear. The insurance industry, like so many others in today's society, has experienced fundamental structural changes and will never return to "the good old days." It is inevitable that companies will consolidate. Unfortunately, many companies will wait too long to consolidate from a position of strength. The following chapters tell the story of two companies that did consolidate in what they called an affiliation from a position of strength.

HOW WE ASSEMBLED THE STORY

We began gathering information for this book in the spring of 1992. Our sources included over 100 interviews with members of the two organizations and others who helped in the affiliation process. We also examined hundreds of memoranda, reports, meeting minutes, and company publications. At all stages of our exploration, we were more concerned with the quality and completeness of our research than we were with its speed. Therefore, it has taken us a long while to complete this book. So long, in fact, that some things have changed as we went along, and we have had to go back and alter our manuscript to make it reflect the current state of the affiliation. Even as we write, the affiliation continues to evolve, and the reader should understand that what we have described was up-to-date as of April 1995.

OUR INTENDED AUDIENCES

It is our hope that several groups might benefit by reading this volume. First, we believe the employees of the affiliated companies will enjoy the documentation of what is for many of them a major event in their lives.

Second, we think executives, managers, and change agents who are members of, or consultants to, organizations that are immersed in, or considering, large-scale change may find useful what we have written.

Third, students of organizational change may find our story interesting as a description of a major organizational transformation and the challenges and opportunities such an undertaking presents.

THE CONTENTS OF THIS VOLUME

We begin by placing our story in context. Chapter 2 is intended to provide that context by offering a review of the literature on the human side of large-scale organizational change, including instances in which companies merge or affiliate. This literature will lay a foundation for an understanding of the human issues involved when companies join and will allow us to highlight special aspects of the process we will explore in later chapters.

In Chapter 3, we will detail the histories of the two companies involved. In addition, we will describe their preaffiliation cultures in order to prepare the reader to understand the description of the integration of those cultures.

In Chapter 4, we will describe the tumultuous changes that occurred in the financial services industry in the 1970s and 1980s. It was these circumstances, as well as some conditions particular to CUNA Mutual and Century Companies, that led them to consider alternative ways of managing themselves.

Chapter 5 will make clear the alternatives considered by each of the companies, the reasons for selecting to affiliate with another company, and the way in which they found each other.

Chapter 6 describes the methods the two organizations used to learn about each other, including the informal meetings between various managers, the due diligence process, the meetings of the boards of directors of the two companies, and the several approval steps that were necessary involving policy-owners and regulatory groups.

In Chapter 7 we describe the nature of the affiliation, the form and structure of the joint marketing effort (called Plan America), and the beginning steps of the integration process, including the early joint management meetings and integrating the investment and legal departments, which were the first two departments involved in the functional integration of the two organizations.

In Chapter 8 we will describe the ongoing process of searching for and implementing steps to optimize the potential synergies between the organizations, including the movement of people between the companies, integration of human resource management policies and systems, information processing systems, marketing and distribution systems, and the challenge of management succession planning for the affiliated companies.

In our final chapter, we will share with the reader the lessons learned in the affiliation process by summarizing what has gone well and what could have gone better and why we think it has been so. We will relate what we have learned to the general literature on the human aspects of mergers and affiliations discussed in Chapter 2 and conclude by offering a series of recommendations that will be of use to participants in and students of such undertakings.

Throughout this book the reader will note that we have emphasized the human aspects of our story. That is, we have focused, as we mentioned earlier, on the ways in which people's lives are affected when their companies undergo major change. In Chapter 2 we will review the literature on the human aspects of organizational combinations. We were quite surprised at the number of otherwise comprehensive treatments of the subject of merger and acquisition activity which completely, or almost completely, ignore human issues. In such titles as *The Mergers and Acquisitions Handbook* (Rock, 1987), human issues are briefly touched on and then only in a section called "After the Merger," and in *The Handbook of Mergers, Acquisitions and Buyouts* (Lee and Coleman, 1981), just 22 of its 747 pages are devoted to human considerations. This is particularly noteworthy because in many of the sources we will cite in Chapter 2, it is pointed out that when mergers fail, and about 50 percent of them do, it is more often a result of problems of human incompatibility or poor human resource management than any other causes, and this has been known at least since the late 1960s (see Kitching, 1967; and Davis, 1968).

For this reason, if for no other, we hope the reader will find our story valuable.

REFERENCES

Cass, E. S. 1993. Plugging the surplus drain: Putting expenses under the microscope. *Resource,* February, 20–22.

Davis, R. 1968. Compatibility in corporate marriages. *Harvard Business Review,* 46, July/August.

Kitching, J. 1967. Why do mergers miscarry? *Harvard Business Review,* 45, November /December.

Lee, S. J. & Coleman, R. D., Eds. 1981. *The handbook of mergers, acquisitions and buyouts.* Englewood Cliffs, N.J.: Prentice-Hall.

Rock, M. L. Ed. 1987. *The mergers and acquisitions handbook.* N.Y.: McGraw-Hill.

Shannon, R. 1993. Trends shaping the future of the life insurance industry today. *Journal of the American Society of CLU and ChFC,* May, 16–21.

Stein, R. 1994. Is the industry out of the doldrums at last? *National Underwriter,* January 31, 5–7.

2

Human Issues in Organizational Change

INTRODUCTION

In this chapter we will review and summarize the literature on the human issues involved when organizations undergo massive change. We will focus on the implications of organizational mergers, however, we have found it instructive to include some of the work on other forms of organizational change as well. It is our intention that this review provide a context for the story to follow, and we will return in subsequent chapters to many of the points made here.

We will review literature of two types. The first concerns what is known about the human and psychological implications of organizational mergers and acquisitions. This is the category that is most directly related to the situation which forms the basis for our story. The second category concerns the human and psychological implications of large-scale organizational change (Mohrman, 1989), or organizational transformation (Kilman & Covin, 1989), no matter what form such changes may take. After thoroughly searching the literature, we became convinced that this second category, though more general, offered valuable insight into our understanding of what has taken place in the CUNA Mutual-Century Companies affiliation.

To understand our thinking on this point, it is instructive to explain our concept of large-scale organizational change. We mean by this term any organization-wide change, such as a fundamental change in an organization's culture, a basic shift in management style, or a broad reorganization. Mohrman (1989), defines large-scale organization change as "a lasting change in the character of an organization that significantly alters its performance" (p. 2). This definition comprises two important features, a change in character and a change in performance. It also specifies that the alterations are not temporary and that the organization becomes and remains different. Kilman & Covin's (1989) concept of organizational transformation may also help to understand our view of the phenomenon under discussion here. They define transformation as "a system-wide change in an organization that demands new ways of perceiving, thinking and behaving by all its members" (p. 14). It is our contention that it is useful to think of situations in which one organization merges with or is acquired by another one as special cases of large-scale organizational change or of organizational transformation.

ORGANIZATIONAL CHANGE AND SEPARATION ANXIETY

One useful way to understand the psychological implications of large-scale organizational change is to conceptualize them as having to do with separation anxiety (Astrachan, 1990). When organizations change, something is, in fact, lost: the past. This may take many forms. For example, if one organization merges with another, the name of the organization may change. This may seem to be a rather minor issue, and for many people it is inconsequential. However, for some, the name of their organization is of special significance. One of the organizations in our story had changed its name, in 1985, from Lutheran Mutual Life Insurance to Century Companies of America. This change alone, though it was not part of what we now think of as large-scale organizational change, caused a significant sense of loss on the part of some members of the Lutheran Mutual Life organization. They felt it indicated a move away from the principles upon which the company had been founded.

When broader and more fundamental change is undertaken, the sense of loss and its attendant anxiety, may be more pervasive. So, when the organizational culture changes, some people feel a kind of anomie and rootlessness that are connected to an uncertainty about how to behave. All they are sure of is that there are new expectations, even though they are not certain exactly what those expectations are. Under such conditions, it is common to long for the "good old days" in which things, even if one did not always like them, were unambiguous. Astrachan (1990) suggests that the anxiety experienced in these situations can be best understood as analogous to what takes place whenever one experiences a loss, or even expects to experience a loss, that is, separation anxiety.

Most of the research on separation anxiety has been done with animals, (e.g., Harlow's 1971 work with primates) or with children, and there has been very little written on separation anxiety at the group level (exceptions would include Levinson, 1970 and 1972). However, Astrachan (1990) feels, and we agree, that the concept of separation anxiety may be helpful in understanding some of the behavior often observed in merger and acquisition situations.

Separation anxiety is a distinctive anxiety associated with the fear of having a relationship change drastically or end. It is the cognitive emotional state caused by cues of impending separation. It commences before the separation actually takes place and can, in fact, occur when separation is only implied or rumored. For example, unplanned and/or unexpected changes in behavior can set it off. One normally thinks of separation anxiety as connected to changes in interpersonal relationships, but we feel it is instructive in trying to understand organizational change, to expand our view to include organizational separation. That is, we are suggesting that it may be that when large-scale organizational change takes place, some people may feel that it ruptures their connections to many aspects of their environment. Bridges (1988) suggests that some people react negatively to large-scale organizational change in order to, "legitimate and protect their identities, their sense of meaning, their world" (p. 8).

In preparing the material for this book, we identified many examples of separation anxiety behavior on the part of members of both of the organizations involved. One story which illustrates a variety of such behaviors involves the integration of the investment functions of Century and CUNA Mutual. We will tell this story more completely in later chapters, but at this point, we can say that the Century investment people (who moved as a group from the Century offices in Waverly, Iowa, to the CUNA Mutual offices in Madison, Wisconsin) tried to minimize their sense of loss by essentially recreating the familiar Century culture within the CUNA Mutual organization. The fact that their leader, who had led the Century investment group, was appointed to lead the combined investment functions, made this possible. Some of the CUNA Mutual investment people, for their part, reacted to the loss of their culture as predicted by Astrachan (1990), who suggests that suspicion and fearfulness, denial, strong feelings of insecurity, overt hostility and aggressiveness, and withdrawal and depression are all characteristic of separation anxiety. Similar reactions to loss of culture appeared on the part of some of the staff in Waverly and particularly among members of the Century career system. Astrachan also suggests that people working in groups and experiencing separation anxiety sometimes work poorly, specifically that they tend to engage in a kind of "groupthink." Research by Buono & Nichols (1985) describes similar findings, as does the work of Marks & Mirvis (1986). In addition, there is an excellent and illuminating treatment of this subject by Buono & Bowditch (1989).

It may be useful to note that it is common when people feel they may be losing something valuable to them, to create a situation in which they (unconsciously) will be able to minimize their sense of loss. One way to accomplish this is to become hostile. It is often easier to separate from someone or something with whom or which you are angry than to separate when your only feelings are of loss and devastation. Anger allows one to feel that the situation was not very good anyway and that makes the inevitable separation easier. In the case of a large-scale organizational change, we may, in this light, be able to see some of the resentment and hostility that is directed at members of upper management as functional in that it may help people to accept the new situation.

On the other hand, Astrachan (1990) also points out that there are other behaviors that may arise from separation anxiety that actually work to retard the progress of the organizational change. Perhaps his best example is one in which he describes a situation in which people feel strongly attached to their organization, and may even have have joined it, in part, to establish and maintain strong, stable attachments. He suggests that in such a situation, when those attachments appear to be threatened, we might expect some people to sabotage the change unconsciously by, for example, choosing incompetent replacements in order to provide an excuse for key people to remain in place, or by lowering productivity, or by obstructing communication, or by delving into great detail and overanalyzing decisions if they feel that rapid and successful work may actually aid in achieving the separation.

ORGANIZATIONAL CHANGE AND EXPECTATIONS

Even if people do not suffer separation anxiety when their organizations combine, their psychological contracts (Levinson, 1970, 1972) may be violated and, if so, dysfunctional attitudes and behaviors are likely to emerge. It is common for there to be changes in people's understanding of what they can expect from their organizations and, if these changes evolve slowly, most people can accomodate them. However, in large-scale change that occurs rapidly there may be significant and sudden shifts that produce a sharp discrepancy between what employees have come to expect and the realities they encounter. Pritchett (1985) presents a similar picture in his volume entitled *After the Merger: Managing the Shockwaves*.

The extent to which people are dissatisfied by the changes that occur may also be a function of their perceived relative level of deprivation. Crosby (1984) says that relative deprivation theory indicates that "feelings of deprivation depend on the joint occurrence of frustrated wants and violated entitlements" (p. 51). Thus, employees feel a sense of deprivation when the change creates the impression that they are somehow worse off than they were before the change, or than they feel they would have been if the change had not taken place. In the case of the CUNA Mutual-Century Companies affiliation, there is no question that some members of each of the organizations felt exactly this, perhaps most clearly illustrated by the reactions of some members of Century Companies' field sales force. (See Chapters 6 and 8.)

A PUNCTUATED EQUILIBRIUM MODEL OF ORGANIZATIONAL CHANGE

Another way to understand large-scale organizational change and people's reactions to it is illustrated by the work of Gersick (1991), who has suggested that the punctuated equilibrium paradigm of change may be more applicable to a variety of fields than the Darwinian gradualism model. Her premise is that there are important commonalities in the way many systems, including human ones, change. She cites research from the fields of individual adult development (Levinson, 1978, 1986), group development (Gersick, 1988, 1989, 1991), organizational evolution (Tushman & Romanelli, 1985, 1986), the history of science (Kuhn, 1970), evolutionary biology (Eldredge & Gould, 1972) and self-organizing systems (Prigogine & Stengers, 1984) to illustrate her point. She asserts that, until recently, the dominant paradigm of evolution has been "Darwin's model of evolution as a slow stream of small mutations, gradually shaped by environmental selection into novel forms" (p. 10).

On the other hand, the punctuated equilibrium paradigm suggests that evolution occurs in the form of "relatively long periods of stability (equilibrium), punctuated by compact periods of qualitative, metamorphic change, (revolution)" (p. 12). In this paradigm, "the interrelationship of these two modes is explained through the construct of a highly durable underlying order or deep structure. It is this deep structure that persists and limits change during equilibrium periods, and that disassembles, reconfigures, and enforces wholesale transformation during revolutionary punctuations" (p. 12). Gersick goes on to suggest that "It is important to note that human systems in equilibrium may look turbulent enough to mask the stability of the underlying deep structure" (p. 18).

We feel that this concept of deep structure is especially helpful in understanding organizational change in general and our story in particular. For example, during the several years preceding the affiliation between CUNA Mutual and Century Companies, a number of significant changes occurred in each of the two companies that may have been perceived at the time as "revolutionary" by at least some members of the organization, but, in retrospect, would probably be better described as examples of what Tushman & Romanelli (1985) call "incremental change during a convergent period." A list of the changes that occurred in Century Companies (most of which we will discuss in more detail in later chapters) would include

1. The construction of a new, and very different, home office building.
2. The company name change, mentioned earlier, from Lutheran Mutual Life to Century Companies of America.
3. A significant change in the way in which the company dealt with the issue of policy loans, such that, if policyholders chose to borrow against their life insurance policies, the loan would henceforth be reflected in the dividends paid.
4. The establishment of a stock subsidiary called Century Life Insurance Company.
5. A major re-examination of the company's approach to managing its surplus.
6. A major changeover in the senior management level that included the retirement or departure of eight executive officers.
7. A three-phase downsizing that resulted in a staff reduction of approximately 25 percent.

In the case of CUNA Mutual, there were also a number of changes. Examples would include the following

1. The establishment of a relationship with National Liberty Marketing, Inc. in which some marketing and insurance functions of CUNA Mutual were "outsourced."
2. The establishment, during the 1970s and 1980s, of a number of new subsidiaries and services for credit unions and their members.
3. The acquisition of the League Companies, which had been owned by the Michigan Credit Union League.
4. The retirement of the company's long-time and very popular CEO and his replacement by a new, and more change-oriented, leader.
5. The reorganization of the company into strategic business units, each responsible for specific lines of business, from individual life and health to corporate property and casualty.
6. The development and establishment of Mutualink, a software system that links credit unions to CUNA Mutual's mainframe computer.
7. The undertaking of a series of construction projects in which, over a period of years, the company built and moved into a new and modern complex of buildings.
8. Introduction of a direct response and a "face-to-face" selling system within the group marketing structure.

Each of these changes was a significant departure from past practice in these companies, but none of them, with the possible exception of CUNA Mutual's business unit reorganization and outsourcing some functions, altered the organizations' deep structures. From the perspective of the punctuated equilibrium paradigm, then, this period of time would best be described as a convergent period. Gersick (1991, p. 17) reports that Tushman and Romanelli (1985) define convergent periods as " Relatively long time spans of incremental change and adaptation which elaborate structure, systems ,controls and resources toward increased coalignment [which] may or may not be associated with effective performance. [They are] characterized by duration, strategic orientation, [and] turbulence. During [these] periods, inertia increases and competitive vigilance decreases; structure frequently drives strategy."

The notion that during convergent periods strategy is driven by structure may be used to identify the essential difference between the changes listed above that took place in the companies and the onset of a "compact period of metamorphic change" represented by the undertaking of the affiliation, which did, in fact, change the deep structure of both organizations and in which, as we shall discuss in detail later, strategy drove structure.

TRANSITION-WORTHY ORGANIZATIONS

For years most of the literature on the basic process of organizational change was based on Lewin's (1951) classic three-phase model of unfreezing, changing, and refreezing. More recently, however, it has become clear that the third phase of Lewin's model, if it ever was descriptive of reality, is no longer. Most of the organizations with which the authors are familiar, and certainly all of those in the financial services industry, simply cannot afford to be "frozen," if that implies static and inflexible. They are operating in conditions of continually shifting environmental demands or what has been described as "continuous white water."

Recent business history is replete with examples of companies that have toppled from the ranks of the most respected as a result of their inability to respond to changes in environmental conditions. As reported in *Business Week* in 1984, twelve of Peters and Waterman's (1982) excellent companies had suffered significant declines in just those two years as a result of their failure to adapt to market changes. Since 1984, several other companies that had been focused on in *In Search of Excellence* have also fallen on hard times, including Boeing, Hughes Aircraft and, perhaps most surprisingly, IBM. These organizations evidently were not what Senge (1990) called "learning organizations." That is, though they had histories of success, they lacked what Bridges (1988) has called "transition worthiness".

When the leaders of the two companies in our story set about bringing their respective companies together, they knew they would need to build a transition-worthy organization precisely because they knew that the affiliated organization was going to be in a condition of ambiguity and change for a considerable period of time. This was because they had opted for a process in which strategy would precede structure, which meant that the form the affiliated organization would take would remain unclear, probably for a period of years. Bridges (1988) defines transition worthiness as "an organization's built-in ability to make rapid changes without undue distress and disruption." (p. 84), and he suggests that this is the hallmark of corporate excellence. He suggests that transition worthiness includes two qualities. The first he calls responsive awareness, by which he means the organization's dynamic and open relationship with its changing external environment. The second he labels purposeful flexibility, which is the organization's ability to reconfigure itself while still remaining purposive. Both of these notions will have applicability to our story, but it may serve us to mention at this point that Bridges indicates that purposeful flexibility sometimes requires maintaining a higher staffing level than the currently fashionable "lean and mean" style would recommend. This point will be used in later chapters to illustrate one of the differences between the Century Companies and CUNA Mutual cultures.

A final comment on the concept of transition-worthy organizations concerns Bridges' assertion that such organizations are ones in which change is viewed as the rule rather than the exception, in which change does not call out survival behavior but learning behavior, and in which control refers not to keeping everything in place but to keeping things in rhythm and balance. We mention this here because it is exactly that kind of atmosphere that the two corporate leaders in our story set out to create as they brought their organizations together. The challenges they faced in achieving that lofty goal will become evident as our story unfolds.

THE ROLE OF TOP MANAGEMENT

Thus far, we have tried to make it clear that we are conceptualizing the affiliation of CUNA Mutual and Century Companies as a special case of system-wide organizational change. We need also to point out that the role of top management in such a transformation differs from its role in the case of smaller, less pervasive changes. Kilman and Covin (1989) suggest that, "during convergent periods [the role of top management] focuses on maintaining congruence and fit within the organization, because strategy, structure, processes and systems are fundamentally sound. The myriad incremental substantive decisions can be delegated to middle level management which possess the needed expertise and information" (p. 125). Thus, during convergent periods top management's role involves maintaining the organization's emphasis on strategy, mission and core values, and being vigilant for changes in the environment which may present opportunities or challenges.

However, during large-scale change, or what Kilmann and Covin (1989) refer to as frame-breaking change, direct executive involvement is required. They say, "Given the enormity of this kind of change and the internal forces that make for inertia, executive leadership must be involved in the specification of strategy, structure and organizational processes as well as in the development of implementation plans. During frame-breaking change executive leadership must be directly involved in reorienting the organization whereas convergent change can be delegated" (p. 164). Tichy and Ulrich (1984) describe a similar skill set and label it "transformational leadership." As we will describe in later chapters, both of the Chief Executive

Officers (CEOs) in our story worked hard to provide strong, direct leadership during the protracted period of planning for and implementating the affiliation of their companies. During some stages of the affiliation process the Century CEO's management style became noticeably different than it had been, and this created some difficulties for some of his people, which we will describe at a later point.

One additional aspect of the role of top management should be noted at this point. It has to do with the issue of how much control of the process of organizational change is reasonable. Most of the executives we know prefer situations in which they feel able to exercise a substantial amount of control. This usually takes the form of predictability, that is, most of them do not like surprises. Buono and Bowditch (1989), in their book *The Human Side of Mergers and Acquisitions*, discuss what they call the "illusion of managerial control" during times in which organizations are combining. They suggest that once the intention to merge with another firm is announced, certain changes are inevitable and that among these is a "breakdown in normal business processes and activities." They argue that there are simply too many things to manage during such periods and that some of them are, inevitably, going to be beyond management's control, but that "the fact that complete control is lacking does not mean that no control is possible" (p. 78). Buono and Bowditch (1989) report that their studies have convinced them that it is virtually impossible to prevent people's fears, uncertainties, stresses, and tensions from emerging and impossible to stop them from disrupting organizational processes. Consequently, they feel that an important executive skill in such situations is the ability to differentiate between the controllables and the uncontrollables and to identify the areas that can be managed in the traditional sense and those that must be managed through what they call coping strategies.

Mirvis and Marks (1992) also offer the opinion that even in the friendliest and best managed instances of organizational combination, they have observed what they call the "merger syndrome." They suggest that as soon as the merger (or affiliation) is announced, the following sequence of phenomena will occur among a substantial portion of the organizations' members: (1) preoccupation, (2) imagining the worst, (3) stress reactions including aggressiveness and withdrawal, (4) crisis management, (5) constricted communication, (6) the illusion of control among top management, and then, as the two organizations begin to combine, (7) the clash of cultures, (8) the we-versus-they syndrome, (9) superior and/or inferior views of each other's organization, (10) attack and defend behavior, (11) a win or lose philosophy in interactions with each other, and (12) decisions by coercion, horse trading and default.

Some of the most recent suggestions for overcoming some of these problems have to do with what we consider rather heavy-handed approaches to accomplishing organizational change. One example is Tichy and Sherman's (1993) description of Jack Welch's remaking of the General Electric organization. A second, and even more extreme example is Pritchett and Pound's (1993) handbook for managers entitled, *High-Velocity Culture Change*, in which the authors write, "Watching a corporate culture change is like walking through a war zone. You see misery. Wreckage. Trauma. And casualties" (p. 22).

This is, obviously, not a very pretty or optimistic picture and we have included this material not because the CUNA Mutual-Century Companies story clearly illustrates all of these phenomena, although some difficulties certainly occurred, but because we will try to show, in Chapter 9, some ways in which at least some of these difficulties can be avoided or minimized. We agree with Pritchett and Pound's assertion that, "Trying not to disturb people, seeking to appease everybody by taking it slow and easy, can be the cruelest move of all" (p. 8), but we also feel it is unecessary to create havoc.

ORGANIZATIONAL CULTURE

When the early discussions between the two CEOs were taking place, both had the impression that the cultures of their respective organizations were quite similar. As we look back now, with the advantage of several years' perspective, it is evident that the two CEOs overestimated the extent of the overlap. There were in fact several similarities in the two companies, but if these had anything to do with organizational culture, it was more related to what Buono and Bowditch (1989) have called objective culture than to what they refer to as subjective culture. Objective culture refers to the artifacts created by an organization. Examples would include physical settings of buildings, office locations and decor, dress styles, and so on. Subjective organizational culture refers to the pattern of beliefs, assumptions, and expectations shared by members of the organization, along with their general way of perceiving the organization's environment and its values, norms, and role requirements. To further illustrate our point, it was obvious that both companies put a very high value, as mutual insurance companies, on return to their policyholders (an objective cultural example.) At the same time, it later became apparent that the management styles of the two companies were quite different (a subjective cultural example.) Buono and Bowditch (1989) suggest "Both aspects of culture are important for a full understanding of a particular organization. Subjective organizational culture, however, typically provides a more dictinctive basis for characterizing and interpreting similarities and differences among people in different firms. While objective culture may show similarities across organizations, subjective organizational culture is more specific to a particular enterprise." (p. 139)

While it would be an exaggeration to describe the cultures of CUNA Mutual and Century Companies as having "collided" in the way that the organizations in Buono, Bowditch, and Lewis's (1985) case examples did, there is no doubt that the differences in their cultures generated some challenges to their successful integration. We will expand on the subject of integrating organizational cultures and the attendant challenges when we describe in detail the nature of the two companies in Chapter 3.

REFERENCES

Astrachan, J. 1990. *Mergers, acquisitions and employee anxiety.* New York: Praeger.
Bridges, W. 1988. *Surviving corporate transition.* New York: Doubleday.
Buono, A., and Bowditch, J. 1989. *The human side of mergers and acquisitions.* San

Francisco: Jossey-Bass.

Buono, A., Bowditch, J., & Lewis, J. 1985. When cultures collide: The anatomy of a merger. *Human Relations, 38*, 477–500.

Buono, A., and Nichols, L. 1985. *Corporate policy, values and social responsibility.* New York: Praeger.

Business Week, November 5, 1984. "Who's excellent now?" 76–88.

Crosby, F. 1984. Relative deprivation in organizational settings. In B. M. Staw(ed.) *Research in organizational behavior, Vol. 6.* Greenwich, Conn.: JAI Press.

Eldredge, N. and Gould, S. (1972). Punctuated equilibria: An alternative to phyletic gradualism. In T. J. Schopf (ed.), *Models in paleobiology.* San Francisco: Freeman, Cooper & Co.

Gersick, C. 1988. Time and transition in work teams: Toward a new model of group development. *Academy of Management Journal 31*, 9–41.

Gersick, C. 1989. Marking time: Predictable transitions in task groups. *Academy of Management Journal 32*, 274–309.

Gersick, C. 1991. Revolutionary change theories: A multilevel exploration of the punctuated equilibrium paradigm. *Academy of Management Review 16*, 10–36.

Gersick, C. & Hackman, R. 1990. Habitual routines in task-performing groups. *Organizational behavior and human decision processes 47*, 65–97.

Harlow, H. 1971. *Learning to love.* San Francisco: Albion.

Kilman, R.L. & Covin, T.J. 1989. *Corporate Transformation.* San Francisco: Jossey-Bass.

Kuhn, T. S. 1970. *The structure of scientific revolution.* Chicago: Univ. of Chicago Press.

Levinson, D. J. 1978. *The seasons of a man's life.* New York: Knopf.

Levinson, D.J. 1986. A conception of adult development. *American Psychologist 41*, 3–13.

Levinson, H. 1970. A psychologist diagnoses merger failures. *Harvard Business Review 48*, 139–147.

Levinson, H. 1972. Easing the pain of personal loss. *Harvard Business Review 50*, 41–54.

Lewin, K. 1951. *Field Theory in Social Science.* New York: Harper & Row.

Marks, M. L. & Mirvis, P. H. 1986. Merger syndrome. *Psychology Today*, October, 36–42.

Mirvis, P. H. & Marks, M. L. 1992. *Managing the merger: making it work.* Englewood, N.J.: Prentice-Hall. New York: Bantam.

Mohrman, A. M. 1989. *Large scale organizational change.* San Francisco: Jossey-Bass.

Peters, T. J. & Waterman, R. H. 1982. *In search of excellence.* New York: Harper & Row.

Prigogine, I. & Stengers, I. 1984. *Order out of chaos: Man's new dialogue with nature.* New York: Bantam.

Pritchett, P. 1985. *After the merger: Managing the shockwaves.* Homewood, Ill.: Dow Jones-Irwin.

Pritchett, P. & Pound, R. 1993. *High-velocity culture change.* Dallas: Pritchett.

Senge, P. 1990. *The fifth discipline: The art and practice of the learning organization.* New York: Doubleday.

Tichy, N. & Sherman, S. 1993. *Control your destiny or someone else will.* New York: Doubleday.

Tichy, N. & Ulrich, B. 1984. The leadership challenge: a call for the transformational leader. *Sloan Management Review, 24*, 59–68.

Tushman, M., Newman, W. & Romanelli, E. 1986. Convergence and upheaval: Managing the unsteady pace of organizational evolution. *California Management Review 29*, 29–44.

Tushman, M. & Romanelli, E. 1985. Organizational evolution: A metamorphosis model of convergence and reorientation. In L. Cummings & B. Staw (Eds.). *Research in organizational behavior, Vol. 7.* Greenwich, Conn.: JAI Press.

3

Histories of the Companies and Descriptions of Their Preaffiliation Cultures

INTRODUCTION

Now that we have reviewed the literature on large-scale organizational change in general and on the psychological aspects of mergers/acquisitions in particular, we offer profiles of CUNA Mutual and Century Companies to help in understanding the challenges in combining the two organizations. We will discuss each of the companies separately by giving a synopsis of its history and an outline of its pre-affiliation culture. Then we will offer a summary of the major cultural differences that existed between the companies before the affiliation. We will be discussing the implications of these differences in upcoming chapters. In summarizing the histories of the two organizations, we have relied heavily on company histories that had been previously compiled. (See references at the end of this chapter.)

THE HISTORY OF CUNA MUTUAL

The CUNA (Credit Union National Association) Mutual Insurance Society was formed in 1935. To understand its role, the reader must have a rudimentary understanding of the credit union movement out of which the society emerged. A credit union provides services similar to those offered by a bank. However a credit union is a financial *cooperative* which is owned by its members and controlled through a democratic process based on one member-one vote. There are no stockholders in a credit union. If there are any profits, they are returned to the members in the form of dividends or expanded services.

The notion of serving people's financial needs through a cooperative took shape in a small town in Germany in the 1850s in the mind of one Friedrich Raiffeisen. He was the town's mayor and he formed a "credit association" to help the farmers in the area survive. The spread of such cooperative associations in Europe was slow but steady.

Around the turn of the century the first credit union in North America was organized. It was in Quebec and representatives of that credit union made a presentation in Boston, in 1908, in which they described their institution as an alternative for poor people who were being preyed upon by loan sharks. That presentation was attended by a prominent Boston department store owner and philanthropist named Edward A. Filene. Filene was impressed with the idea and gave his support, both financially and in terms of his time and effort. Along with Boston attorney Roy Bergengren, Filene developed the credit union idea on a national scale. Their progress was steady but slow until the Great Depression, during which the movement made great strides.

President Roosevelt signed the Federal Credit Union Act into law on June 26, 1934. By then there were 3,000 credit unions in 40 states with nearly 500,000 members. Later that year Bergengren organized a national credit union convention in Estes Park, Colorado, at which the Credit Union National Association (CUNA) was born.

THE NEED FOR INSURANCE

In 1935, at CUNA's first annual meeting, the subject of insurance came up. The problem seemed to be that sometimes a credit union member would take out a loan and then either die or become disabled before the loan had been repaid. In such a case the member's family or cosigners were liable for the unpaid amount. If they could not pay, the credit union absorbed the loss, and, in some cases, the credit unions simply could not afford to do that.

The answer, they decided, was insurance. So in 1935 CUNA Mutual was formed, using a $25,000.00 loan from Filene. The delegates to that first meeting also decided to locate both CUNA and CUNA Mutual in Madison, Wisconsin.

The first CUNA Mutual product was individual credit life insurance, which was sold to credit union members, who paid for the policies themselves. Later in its first year, the company introduced group credit life insurance, which it named Loan Protection Insurance and on which the credit union paid the premium. This rapidly became one of the strongest selling points for credit unions; that is, if a person were to borrow money from a bank, it would cost extra to protect it, but if the money were borrowed from a credit union, the protection would be offered at no cost to the borrower. In 1936, the company added loan protection against disability, which was a great advantage to workers in the 1930s, and, in 1938, to encourage saving, it introduced Life Savings Insurance, paid for by the credit union. In the late 1960s and early 1970s the company introduced commercial property and casualty insurance and fidelity bonds into its portfolio. Individual life and property/casualty coverages were added as the company developed its interest in selling directly to credit union members.

Continuing Development

From 1936 to 1941 credit union membership grew from 1.1 million to 3.3 million and the new company grew rapidly along with the credit union movement. By 1941, CUNA Mutual was providing over $100 million in coverage which was being sold by mail and by word of mouth through the credit union movement. There was no sales force. World War II brought this growth to a temporary halt, but after the war the growth pattern resumed. In 1950, President Harry Truman set the cornerstone in the new headquarters of CUNA and CUNA Mutual in Madison and this event helped bring national attention to the credit union movement. Today, in 1995, there are over 36,000 credit unions in seventy-nine countries with more than 87 million members and total assets of over 240 billion dollars.

CUNA Mutual has grown to a company approaching 5,000 employees, and it is the leading writer of credit life insurance in the world. In addition, the company provides many services to credit unions in areas such as technology, youth and retirement services, and general promotion of the credit union movement. Combined with Century Companies, the two organizations have assets of over $5.2 billion and a total of more than $93.2 billion of insurance in force.

CUNA MUTUAL'S PREAFFILIATION CULTURE

The Credit Union as the Customer

It is probably impossible to overstate the influence that the idea "The credit union is our customer" has within the CUNA Mutual organization. As will be evident in the paragraphs to follow, this idea pervades virtually everything this organization does, including the ways in which people typically interact in the company.

Interpersonal Style

CUNA Mutual could be characterized as an organization with a high degree of market sensitivity. That is to say, it is an organization in which a great deal of attention is given to insuring that any decision or action taken will benefit its market. Included in the marketplace are, of course, the individual credit union executives, as well as the credit union leagues and their representatives and those members of the marketplace who were also members of the CUNA Mutual Board of Directors. This market sensitivity has been in evidence in a number of ways. For example, it sometimes occurred during meetings at CUNA Mutual that someone would question a suggestion by saying, "Have we given full consideration to the likely market reaction?" At times, decisions or actions might be delayed in order to do a full assessment of the market impact. There was an important historical reason for CUNA Mutual to be especially sensitive to its relationship to its market. As we discussed earlier, CUNA Mutual was, quite literally, a *creation* of the credit union movement and, as such, had become almost totally dependent for its survival on that market. As we get further into our story, the reader will see exactly how this relationship influenced the affiliation with Century Companies. At this point, it is important to understand that it was, and remains, of paramount importance in the minds of most CUNA Mutual managers that they keep asking themselves how a given decision might be viewed by their customer, the credit union movement.

It may also be useful to note that this sensitivity to the credit union marketplace seems to have developed into a general environment within CUNA Mutual, which is characterized by a higher degree of concern for maintaining smooth running relationships than was true in Century Companies. As we shall see in later chapters, this became a challenge for those trying to integrate the CUNA Mutual and Century Companies cultures.

Influence of the Credit Union "Movement"

A second, and closely related, aspect of the CUNA Mutual culture concerns the term, "credit union *movement*." The movement had its roots as a social cause to help the disadvantaged help themselves. Many people within CUNA Mutual still have very strong feelings concerning the importance of the role played in society by credit unions. These feelings go far beyond those one might normally expect people to have about their work. A sense of *mission*, of being a part of something unique and necessary, exists among many CUNA Mutual people. They feel they are providing a set of services to people who might not otherwise have access to those services at all, or who certainly would not have the same quality of access, or the same degree of understanding and responsiveness to their needs.

Relationship with the Board of Directors

CUNA Mutual's relationship with its board of directors has been a unique one. The board is made up primarily of credit union people including league executives and credit union executives and, as such, the board is, quite literally, made up of members of the company's market. In addition, it has been typical for there to be five to seven Board meetings a year, each of several days duration. (This may be the ultimate example of being "close to your customer.") As a result, the board has played a rather active role in the decisions made in the company and has been involved to a much greater degree in the day-to-day operation of the company than would usually be the case in a company of this size.

Type of Business

CUNA Mutual's market strategy of differentiation and focus required that it meet as many of the needs of the credit unions and the credit union leagues as possible. This necessitated providing a wide range of products and services. The result was that CUNA Mutual had become a company that was, in a sense, in the "credit union business," more than it was in the insurance business; that is, it had multiple product lines. It had also become a very powerful force in the credit union market and had, prior to the affiliation, a dominant position in its market that had been achieved, in part, by this willingness to be a product innovator.

In addition, CUNA Mutual's business was experience rated. That is to say, short-term results could be measured and managed. This created a business that was somewhat cyclical, and one in which it was possible to "turn things around" quickly, especially in view of the fact that some of their products had relatively higher profit margins because of their special differentiation.

Influence of the Union

Another aspect of the CUNA Mutual culture which should be mentioned is that a significant number of the employees are members of a labor union. This is, of course, entirely consistent with the general idea of people coming together to meet common needs and/or to increase their influence. In fact, the original suggestion that employees should join a labor union came, in the late 1940s, from then managing director of the company, Thomas W. Doig. He felt it was in the best interests of the employees that they do so and he, therefore, urged just that. If one truly understands the "movement" aspect of the CUNA Mutual culture, this should not be surprising. From the point of view of the affiliation, this meant that with the existence of a union contract, the companies probably would have to take a different approach to integration than they would if a contract had not been in effect.

The Factors of Growth in Size and Geography

At the time of the affiliation CUNA Mutual had over 4,000 employees. The largest number of them, over 2,250, worked at the corporate headquarters in Madison, but there were also over 700 in Canada, 380 in field sales, about 200 in a California office and over 450 in the League Companies in Michigan. It is also of significance that a great many of these people had joined the company since 1970. In that year there were less than 800 employees. In fact, as recently as 1985, there had been just 2,600. This, of course, does not make CUNA Mutual a large organization when it is compared with, say, the Prudential or Metropolitan Life companies. Nevertheless, it does mean that the all-in-the-family feeling that had prevailed when the company was much smaller was no longer present.

In addition, CUNA Mutual operates in over fifty countries, and this, of course, has implications for its internal culture and ways of functioning.

Finally, CUNA Mutual had become a company in which it was commonplace for there to be acquisition activity. That is to say, by the late 1980s, most CUNA Mutual employees had become used to the idea that the company was in a growth mode which involved the acquisition and integration of smaller organizations. This experience contrasted sharply with that of most Century people and we will see shortly how that became a factor in the affiliation.

Leadership Continuity

At the time of the affiliation, CUNA Mutual was undergoing a change in leadership at the top level from a Chief Executive Officer (CEO) who had led the company from 1973 until 1988, to a new leader. The leadership styles of these two men were quite different and, as a result, the uncertainty that almost always accompanies a leadership change was exacerbated. To be sure, the new CEO had exerted a substantial amount of influence in the company for a number of years prior to becoming CEO (he had been a consultant and later a prominent and vigorous officer of the company for some time and had been especially visible as Chief Operating Officer [COO]), and he was, therefore, not an unknown quantity. However, he was known to believe that substantial changes in the company were going to be necessary for it to remain a strong force in the increasingly competitive credit union market. This generated some concern about how his leadership might affect both day-to-day operations and general company strategy. In particular, he had emphasized the importance of "business divisions," and had structured the organization around this concept, which constituted a major change in thinking for most of the CUNA Mutual management and some of them were still struggling with how best to analyze the results at the time of the affiliation.

Opportunity-Seeking/Decision-Making Style

CUNA Mutual was also a company in which decisions were sometimes influenced by the factors outlined earlier (having to do with maintaining a relationship with the market). The CEO liked to describe his (and, he hoped, his company's) opportunity-seeking and management decision making style as similar to that of "a fighter pilot," by which he meant assessing opportunities and determining a course of action in a responsive, fluid rather than a rigid manner, in order to take advantage of rapidly changing business opportunities. Since, as we said above, this executive had had such a broad impact on the entire CUNA Mutual organization, this decision-making style also became a pervasive influence in the organization. When the two companies' management groups came together for a series of get-acquainted meetings beginning in June of 1989, the CUNA Mutual group described its own opportunity-seeking and decision-making style as "More of a fighter pilot style of execution rather than a railroad engineer approach." They described the approach as an opportunistic one in which lengthy, slow-moving cost/benefit analysis was not always possible.

Performance Expectations

In general, the need to perform well in the stock market creates greater external pressures for corporate performance standards in stock insurance companies than do the policyholders in the case of mutual insurance companies. Nevertheless, cost problems and the need to compete have influenced many mutuals. CUNA Mutual, with its intense market focus and market dominance, had not experienced the same degree of pressure as some other mutuals and, as a result, had been able, in some instances, to manage performance expectations with a lighter hand than might have otherwise been the case. But even in CUNA Mutual's case, the possible loss of market dominance required changes in strategy and structure as the company moved into the 1990s.

THE HISTORY OF CENTURY COMPANIES

Origins

A great economic depression in the 1870s left many American families impoverished and seeking protection from complete financial ruin in the event of death of the breadwinner. Among them were many Lutheran parishioners who joined lodges or "secret societies" because of the financial protection they offered. The only alternative, insurance companies, often had premiums that were too expensive for many people. Lutheran pastors condemned their parishioners for joining the lodges, and many of the parishioners responded that they did not care for the lodges' rituals but did need the financial security for their families. So, in 1879, at the assembly of the Iowa Synod held in Maxfield, Iowa, three Lutheran pastors drafted plans for the Mutual Aid Society of the German Lutheran Synod of Iowa and Other States. Since they did not wish to engage in business, the founders clearly stated that the society should remain private to serve solely the German Lutheran Synod. Sixty-two members signed the original charter and each paid $1.00 to fund the start-up. The first "certificate" (life insurance policy) was issued September 24, 1879 in the name of one of the founders, Pastor C. Ide of Iowa City.

Subsequent members were assessed a $1.50 entrance fee and a $.25 certificate fee. The rest of the funding came from interest on investments and from periodic assessments which were based on age: $.45 for twenty to thirty year-olds, $.50 for those thirty to forty, $.65 for forty to fifty year-olds, and $.90 for fifty to sixty year-olds. (Nobody over sixty was accepted for membership.) The only kind of insurance available was a $1,000.00 (whole life) certificate. By the end of 1879, 88 members had joined the society and another 117 joined in 1880. By the society's third general assembly in 1882, membership had grown only to 276 thus the delegates decided it was necessary to promote the growth of the society to ensure its survival. The society incorporated on June 21, 1882, and thereafter began a period of steady growth so that by 1888 there were 1,500 members. The society was now growing by about 10 percent a year.

During those early years the society's "home office" was wherever the secretary of the society happened to live, and when G. A. Grossman was elected secretary in 1899, all the society's books and records (which fit into two wooden crates) were sent to his hometown of Waverly, Iowa, where he ran the organization out of the backroom of an old print shop. The society entered the twentieth century with about 4,000 members in 130 local branches; it also had about $30,000.00 invested and had paid more than $250,000.00 in death benefits. The delegates to the 1902 convention voted to increase the maximum amount of insurance offered to $2,000.00 and to establish a $1.00/year dues to be added to the reserve fund. By 1912, the society had several employees, and in that year the first home office building was constructed in downtown Waverly. It was a two-story, 22 by 60 foot building, and for several years the society used only the first floor and rented out the second.

A Level Premium Fraternal

During the early years of the twentieth century, it became apparent that the founders of the society had lacked the foresight and/or understanding to see that their assessment plan was not going to provide adequate funding as the membership matured. It became evident that, unless a drastic change were undertaken in the method of funding, the society was doomed. In 1916, the executive officers called a special delegate assembly in Waverly at which it was decided to adopt level premium rates for all new certificates. They could not change the assessment rates for the 8,000 people who were already members, but they did establish tables by which members could transfer their old class certificates to the new level premium policies. The change to these rates, however, was not widely accepted by the members and 1916 became one of the society's worst years when 238 new members joined and 257 lapsed or died. Membership problems continued and in 1919 in an attempt to attract and hold members, the society introduced its first Twenty Payment Life, Convertible Term policies and began to offer such options as old age benefits, disability contracts, waiver of premium, and a double indemnity accident clause.

These innovations helped but, by the end of 1921, the society still had only 8,296 members, of which 6,535 were still on the old class certificates. Consequently, in October of 1922 the society hired six "transfer men" who served as traveling agents and visited the local branches to persuade old class members to "transfer" their certificates to the new rate system. These agents were able to produce more transfers in one month than had been received in the previous six years. The next month, the society hired another eight transfer men, and by the end of 1922, almost 2,000 transfers had been processed by the home office. By the summer of 1923, almost all of the remaining old class members had either transferred or lapsed. The society began 1924 totally on the new legal reserve system and began to grow quite rapidly. In that same year, the maximum certificate amount was increased to $10,000.00 and the product line was increased to over a dozen different certificates. The traveling transfer agents had been so successful that the society's officers kept them on after the changeover and even hired a superintendant of agents who built and trained the growing field force.

In April of 1925 the society went over $10 million of insurance in force with almost 9,000 members and, in September of 1929, celebrated its golden anniversary with its first $1 million month. However, the depression began to impact the society in 1931 and its growth rate slowed dramatically. Fortunately, the society's death rate during the depression was lower than expected and its survival was thus assured. By 1935, the society experienced a turnaround and began to grow once again. It had weathered the storm, but because of its governance structure, it began to face other challenges.

The new problem was that many states were attempting to pass legislation that would tax fraternal organizations. In addition, several other laws already on the books in many states restricted fraternals in the areas of beneficiaries, certificate requirements, nonmedicals and juvenile death benefits. Most of these laws were on the books or being considered to safeguard the public from the weaker societies, but Lutheran Mutual Aid Society had to comply with them because it was organized as a fraternal. It should also be pointed out that most fraternals, by nature of their organizational structure, are much more political than are most mutual companies. This was probably an additional influence that caused the society's officers to seek a better means with which to serve the needs of their policyowners.

Reorganization as a Mutual

At the society's 1937 general assembly in Milwaukee, Wisconsin, the delegates unanimously approved a proposal which replaced the society's representative form of governance with a corporate structure. The society moved into a new office building, still in Waverly, and on January 1, 1938, began business under the name of Lutheran Mutual Life Insurance Company. As with the reorganization of 1916, it took a while for the public and the company to adapt to the new structure. New business dropped off during the first year, but in 1939 the company regained the difference and went on to an even greater increase in 1940.

World War II brought major changes to almost all aspects of American society and the insurance industry was no exception. Sales of insurance policies grew along with the increase in marriages and the baby boom. Some new investment possibilities emerged such as War Bonds. On the other hand, war casualties accounted for a substantial portion of the company's death claims (over 39 percent in 1945). As the war died down, Lutheran Mutual agents had to compete with such alternative purchases as cars, home appliances, and new homes that were attracting the money of prospective life insurance buyers. Nevertheless, the company prospered after the war, and almost every year resulted in new sales records being achieved. The first agents' training school was held in December 1946 and fourteen agents from eight states attended. The company greatly expanded its advertising and marketing efforts, and by 1953 the company was ranked 88th out of 650 companies in amount of insurance in force. In that same year, *Best's Reports* showed that Lutheran Mutual had the lowest lapse rate, (1.6 percent) of the top 100 companies. By its diamond jubilee in 1954, the company had almost $300 million of insurance in force with $60 million in assets. In 1965 the company passed the milestone of $1 billion of insurance in force. It had taken eighty-seven years to reach this point. The company reached the two billion mark only eight years later, in May of 1974, and the third billion was reached in just four years, by June of 1978.

Recent Changes

In 1970, sensitive to its policyowners' growing needs, Lutheran Mutual Life formed a separate equities corporation and the board of directors adopted an amendment to the company bylaws which permitted the issuance of policies to members of any religious faith. The company still focused to some extent on the Lutheran community but this move opened up new markets as well. In October of the same year, the company purchased a 152-acre tract of land on the west edge of Waverly, which became, and remains, the site of the company's home office. The 80,000- square-foot building was completed in 1977 and additions have expanded it to 130,000 square feet. By the time of its 100th birthday, in 1979, the company employed over 600 people and had almost $600 million in assets.

By 1984, it had become apparent that the company's name no longer reflected the nature of the business. Furthermore, the fraternal companies that had elected to build their distribution systems instead of becoming mutual companies were in a position to "soften" their markets by making significant benevolent contributions, instead of paying heavy taxes as a mutual company. Therefore, the company decided to change its name and began 1985 as Century Life of America. Later a stock subsidiary was organized, and a registered securities broker/dealer, a financial planning firm, and an investment advisory company were established. Together, these companies became known as Century Companies.

CENTURY'S PREAFFILIATION CULTURE

Type of Business

Century had, as has been described above, become somewhat more diversified in its products and services over the decade or so prior to the affiliation. However, by most standards, it remained a fairly typical, rather small mutual insurance company. In that sense, it was a "one product line" company, focusing heavily on life insurance with some ancillary involvement in other financial products and services. To be sure, some of its people, both in the home office and in the field, were more interested in some of the less standard financial products and services, but the company as a whole was not strongly involved in such activities. Century Companies had no choice because of its size and limited resources other than to be a "quick follower" in the market place rather than an innovator.

It may also be important to note that, since its decision to remove itself from identification with the Lutheran market, Century Companies had been operating in an "open" market and, as such, was a small player in that market. That is, they had no sponsored access to the market, and, in fact, no clearly identified and differentiated market at all.

Relationship with Board of Directors

Century's board of directors was made up of business people from a variety of industries, most of whom were not from the insurance field. Several of them had been members of the company's board for some time and felt a strong sense of involvement and ownership for the company and its well-being. It had become fairly common in recent years to have various members of senior management make presentations on topics of current interest in the company at board meetings, so the board members had come to know some of the management people and were in reasonably good touch with the issues facing the company. Nevertheless, their relationship with the company was much more of the standard arms-length type than that which prevailed at CUNA Mutual.

Interpersonal Style

Prior to the affiliation, Century was a company in which organizational politics played a relatively insignificant role. Of course, every organization has *some* politics, but it would be fair to say that at Century they were minimal. This was an issue that had received some considerable attention in the company in the years just prior to the affiliation and substantial progress had been made in creating a working environment in which open, direct communication was the norm. Most members of management felt they could express themselves fairly directly without worrying about how it might affect their careers.

Organizational Size

At the time of the affiliation, Century employed 647 people, of which somewhat less than one-half were in the Waverly, Iowa home office, while the others worked as members of the field distribution system which, while concentrated in the upper midwest, did include offices as far east as Pennsylvania and as far west as Oregon. With only about 300 people in Waverly, it still felt to many employees like a small company and the "family" feeling that had prevailed through most of the company's history, even though it had grown, had been maintained to a remarkable degree. For example, the company continued the tradition of "quarterly updates" which were meetings held in the company cafeteria in which *all* employees of the company received information on the company's financial status. These meetings gave employees the opportunity to ask the company's leadership questions about new initiatives or changes.

Leadership Continuity

Century's CEO had been in his position since 1976, so there was a clear feeling of continuity at the very top. However, the other executives were quite young when compared to most others at their management level. They were all under age forty-five, and had taken over their responsibilities within the few years just prior to the affiliation. Thus, there had been *substantial* leadership change at Century in the years leading up to the affiliation.

Performance Expectations

It is important to note that some of this change in leadership had come as a result of downsizing, and there was a feeling of uncertainty among some of the middle-managers and supervisors concerning the values and likely management style of their leadership group. Century had historically been a somewhat paternalistic company in which hardly anyone ever got fired and in which there was not a particularly high performance expectation. All that had changed in the years just prior to the affiliation. The Century CEO had undertaken to develop what he called a "climate for performance" at Century, and this had resulted in the management of the company focusing much more clearly on performance enhancing activities. Examples included conducting direct, no-nonsense performance reviews, setting clear performance expectations, engaging in job-coaching with marginal performers and increasing expectations concerning hours worked among management, professional, and technical people. As a result, the Century culture had become one in which there was substantially more emphasis on performance than is often the case in mutual insurance companies.

Decision Making Style

Some years before the affiliation, Century had developed what they called a "project management discipline" which consisted of the use of a number of tools and methods to manage the large number of special projects and the task forces associated with them. Century had been forced into this discipline as a result of intense market competition, limited resources and the fact that the company had no clear market niche. An example of this discipline is that they had established an approach to allocating resources to their various projects that involved the activities of two committees that received proposals for projects, decided on allocation of resources, and monitored progress of the projects. This constitutes perhaps the clearest example of the company's general approach to problem solving and decision making; that is to say, Century was a company in which an organized and methodical approach was typically taken when major decisions, projects and problems were faced. There was significant resistance in the company to any attempt to shortcut these carefully planned processes, particularly when decisions on expenditures were involved. This resulted in some decisions being made more slowly than many at CUNA Mutual found comfortable, and this Century Companies characteristic became labeled as being "process oriented" by the CUNA Mutual people, who, as was described above, tended to employ a less methodical approach to decision making.

SUMMARY OF CULTURAL DIFFERENCES

Although careful readers may now be able to form a list of the major differences between the two companies' preaffiliation cultures, we will offer our own below. In doing so, we will focus on those which seemed to us to have the most important implications for the affiliation process that took place between the companies.

	Century	*CUNA Mutual*
Type of business	single-line; book-rated; quick follower	multiple-lines; experience-rated; innovator
Relationship with Board of Directors	arms-length; moderate involvement	very close; high involvement
Interpersonal style	direct, some times confrontational	less direct
Org. size/growth	small; little recent growth	medium; substantial recent growth
Leadership continuity	CEO in place many years; new senior managers	CEO relatively new; most senior managers new
Decision-making style	analytical; process oriented	intuitive; results oriented
Performance expectations	high	moderate
Sensitivity to expenses and costs	high	moderate
Customer focus	low	high

Each of these differences had an impact on the ways in which the two companies came together and we will highlight some of these differences again at the appropriate times in later chapters. It may also be useful to note that there were some similarities between the companies, though not as many as the two CEOs may have thought to be the case during their early discussions. Some of those that came into play were as follows.

1. Both companies were characterized by what one might call a kind of "midwestern, mutual-insurance company ethic." That is, both were concerned with maintaining a relationship with their customers and with their employees that is based on integrity and honesty.

2.   Both companies were led by CEOs who could be chara cterized as "visionaries," who were looking beyond the immediate situations in which their companies found themselves. Both of them were interested in positioning their companies well for the long-term future.
3.   Both companies were financially sound.
4.   Both companies recognized that they lacked important ingredients to secure the type of future they desired. In the CUNA Mutual case, it was individul insurance products, along with the management expertise to market those products. In the Century case, it was a sponsored market.
5.   Both organizations demonstrated a strong commitment to providing high quality products and services for their customers. In both there was significant concern that their offerings constitute good value to their customers.

In considering point 4, it may occur to the reader that Century Companies had actually been in a sponsored market, (Lutherans) for most of its history and that they had given it up and were now seeking to return to such a situation. A brief explanation may be helpful. As we have indicated earlier in this chapter, prior to 1938 Lutheran Mutual was a fraternal insurance company and, for the reasons described above, gave up that status to become a mutual company. One of the important differences between the two types of companies is that fraternals are exempt from federal income taxes since it is assumed that benevolence for the churches will be paid in lieu of taxes. In 1938 federal taxes were not as significant an item for insurance companies as they are today. In effect, that meant that Lutheran Mutual was operating in a sponsored market without the leverage of a benevolence program for their market. At the time of the name change from Lutheran Mutual to Century Companies (1985), the company's CEO asked a senior Lutheran Church official what he thought of when he heard the name Lutheran Mutual. He said he thought, "It's that insurance company in Iowa that never gives us any money." Obviously, the company could not afford to pay significant federal income taxes and at the same time provide benevolent payments to the Lutheran Church and thus the "sponsorship" was not effective.

Most of the factors listed above (both similarities and differences) played a role in the affiliation process and that role will become clear in later chapters. Before describing that process, we will turn in Chapter 4 to a brief description of the conditions that emerged in the insurance industry in the 1980s that caused CUNA Mutual and Century Companies to pursue a number of strategies to remain competitive.

REFERENCES

A century of commitment: Lutheran mutual life. Published by the company in 1979.
The debt shall die with the debtor: The story of the CUNA mutual insurance society. Published by the company in 1991.

4

Structural Change in the Industry

The life insurance business experienced fundamental structural changes during the 1980s and 1990s. Foreign capital, withering margins, and intense competition changed the fundamentals of the business and adapting to change became essential for long-term survival. Schulte (1991) provides a detailed treatment of these issues, and we have relied to some extent on his work to summarize the factors relevant to our story.

PRIOR TO THE 1980s

For the first 100 years plus, the life insurance business was crowded with a relatively large number of companies but experienced none of the normal competitive pressures usually present in such an environment in the free enterprise system. For thirty years prior to 1980, only about 20 percent of the over 1500 companies were serious players, competing for the consumer's purchase of life insurance. The business was not competitive, margins were more than adequate and very few consumers could distinguish as to whether the value of the product they purchased was one of the best. While consumers did not understand the intricacies of the product, they had come to accept the fact that life insurance was a necessary part of their financial plans. In effect, there was an inherent "alliance" between the company and the distribution system, to the disadvantage of the consumer, resulting in a far less efficient delivery of service than is normally found in the free enterprise system. Insurance executives have referred to these early years as the "comfort zone." While there were occasional rate wars they were generally temporary and did not alter the fundamentals of the business.

Life insurance is a long-term purchase and sales illustrations typically focused on results at the end of twenty, thirty, or more years. Over that extended time period, the time value of money can cover the use of high loads. In addition the tax-free accumulation of values was used by many companies to compete with their products as savings vehicles. In this benevolent environment new premiums, assets, reserves, and so on increased and companies built significant capital and surplus accounts. There was very little pressure for management to focus intensely on strategic or tactical plans. Response to the marketplace tended to be more distribution or internally driven than customer driven. Management tended to be functionally oriented and the time line to change products and pricing was frequently measured in years.

Products that were developed were frequently prioritized by the demands of the distribution system. The products were based on what would make for the easiest sale and not based on addressing first what the customer wanted. That is, sales tended to be product or transaction driven rather than needs driven. Sales contests and reward systems also encouraged more of a focus on pushing products than on addressing the needs of the consumer. The basic product lines were Whole Life or some Limited Pay Life, a variety of term policies or riders and annuities. Typically products were illustrated in a rate book and these rate books might be updated every two or three years. Modifications in policy features or in dividend techniques, for example, might take six to nine months to complete as each department function completed its assignment and then passed it on to the next function until the product was ready for delivery to the distribution system. While companies did not have access to data processing techniques until the later years, there was no sense of urgency because the pressure for change was coming from the distribution system and not the consumer and because there was essentially very little pressure on margins.

Because there were very few rate wars during this "wealth accumulation era" that would absorb profits most of the profits went toward the building of home offices and, unfortunately, toward the building of inefficient distribution systems. During these years companies built their organizations by continuing to enhance payout to their distribution systems. In the very early years, first-year commissions were as low as 10 percent increasing currently to 55 percent or as much as 90 percent depending on the type of distribution system. This fact had a significant impact on the "break-even" point for products. To amortize initial expenses including distribution costs it would typically take ten years to "break-even" and nearly twenty years to build sufficient surplus to cover catastrophic losses.

The life insurance business was probably what could be called a sleeping giant, a financial haven. It had its own set of accounting rules which permitted companies to amortize expenses for the acquisition of business over ten or more years, special tax codes designed for the business, and it could offer products that could accumulate tax-free for the consumer prior to withdrawal. Even mediocre management could not keep from being profitable.

THE 1980s AND 1990s

Instead of the "comfort zone," this period has frequently been referred to as the "combat zone." The first shock to the insurance business was in the late 1970s when a Federal Trade Commission (FTC) report stopped just short of recommending to consumers that they should "buy term and invest the difference." The report indicated that the savings component of existing cash-value life insurance was returning less than 2 percent interest to the consumer. While the methodology used by the FTC was challenged the credibility given the report by the press was damaging. In effect the report hurt the sale of permanent insurance and at the same time a price war brought term insurance premiums down and with them agents' commissions.

In addition to the FTC report, by the early 1980s long-term interest rates were running in the high teens with the prime rate reaching as high as 22 percent. Most of the old policies sold carried policy loan interest rates of 6 or 7 percent. When consumers went to local banks for loans, the banks would suggest that the individual go to the insurance company, borrow on the consumer's policy and pay only 6 or 7 percent on the loan. This resulted in a tremendous movement of funds out of the company (referred to as disintermediation). Many companies had money tied up in long term bonds and mortgages that were illiquid. As a result, companies had to borrow money at the bank for 15 percent or more in order to satisfy policyholder loan requests paying six or seven percent.

A significant increase in inflation also had a dramatic effect on the business. The consumer for the first time took an active interest in what had always been a rather complex product—the consumer understood "interest"—especially in an inflationary environment. The consumer began to demand the product that appeared to credit the best rate of interest.

In response to consumer demand, companies developed interest sensitive products such as universal life and variable universal life which were expensive to develop and costly to administer. Furthermore, to be more responsive to the consumer, products had to be developed and delivered in a shorter time frame. The result was that internal expenses increased.

If the agent who sold the original product could not deliver the best rate, consumers changed the policy to another company. In effect, the decline in commissions to the agent because of greater term sales plus consumer demand for a better interest return on their policies forced agents into a new "alliance," one with the policyholder instead of the company.

The insurance companies' distribution systems began to "roll" (that is, change an old policy into a new one) policies that had been sold in previous years into new policies, if not issued by the agent's own company then into a policy of another company. The cost of acquiring these old policies, that were on the books of companies and were now being "rolled," had been amortized so that a greater proportion of the premiums received in the later years would be added to profit. Many companies experienced a decrease in their in-force block of business and a decrease in their surplus. In effect, companies began to lose control of their future.

In addition to a significant increase in administrative costs and a loss of control of distribution systems, there was a significant infusion of foreign capital (buying the stock of smaller companies), which provided additional funds for companies to engage aggressively in the price war, pressure for an increase in taxes from government agencies, and a tendency for regulatory agencies to be slow to respond to the needs of companies. Furthermore, with interest-sensitive products, companies were now in more direct competition with other financial service organizations.

With increasing administrative and acquisition costs, due to both inflation and increased industry complexity, "critical mass" became an issue for the first time. While the numbers of policies in-force decreased, expenses in total to administer those policies increased thus creating pressure to administer more "mass." Furthermore new business issues were flat for the business, and acquisition costs were increasing which forced a focus on "critical mass" for new business. In effect, this resulted in a company focus on transactions or product selling as opposed to the more sustainable process of needs or relationship selling.

In summary, competition was intense, margins were eroding, critical mass became a significant issue for the first time and the necessary surplus to build the business was decreasing. The insurance industry had truly experienced fundamental structural changes. Beginning in Chapter 5, we will detail the story of how Century Companies and CUNA Mutual responded to these changes by coming together.

REFERENCES

Schulte, G. 1991. *The fall of first executive.* New York: Harper.

5

Origins of the Affiliation

INTRODUCTION

Now that we have reviewed the histories of the two companies and characterized their respective preaffiliation cultures, we will detail the events that led up to CUNA Mutual and Century Companies deciding to affiliate. The story is the same for both companies in one sense. That is, both companies were affected by the changing conditions in the insurance industry described in Chapter 4. However, each company responded in its own way to those conditions, as well as to conditions specific to itself, and so their stories are different in many respects as well. Consequently, we will begin by relating two separate stories here, showing how each company worked to maintain its strong position in the face of those changing conditions. We will describe the various steps considered, and sometimes undertaken, by each company, the reasons for selecting the path of affiliating with another company, and the search for suitable partners. Finally, we will bring the two stories together by describing how the chance meeting of the two CEOs occurred and the steps that were taken subsequent to that meeting. We will begin with CUNA Mutual's story.

CUNA MUTUAL'S INTEREST IN THE INDIVIDUAL INSURANCE MARKET

As described in Chapter 3, CUNA Mutual had focused to a large degree on group coverages. Its primary products were credit life and disability insurance sold through credit unions on a group basis to their members, but it also offered property/casualty insurance, employee benefit products, and the fidelity bond. In addition, for many years CUNA Mutual had had an interest in getting into the individual credit union members life insurance market as well. The major reason for this interest was that their group insurance sales were subject to rather wide cyclical variation and they were interested in "smoothing out" their flow of business, achieving diversification of income and greater stability in earnings. Some in the company were also looking ahead to the time when many credit union members might be more interested in other products. As a result, the company had made a number of attempts to enter the area of individual life insurance.

Development of An Agency System

Perhaps the earliest grew out of the activities of a policyowners' advisory committee that had been appointed by company management in 1963. That committee was critical of a lack of expansion in the area of individual life contracts and recommended that an agency system be developed primarily for the sale of individual life and homeowner's contracts. Management accepted the committee's report and CUNA Mutual's Chief Executive Officer (CEO) at the time subsequently appointed a director of agencies and charged him with developing an agency system for CUNA Mutual.

As anyone familiar with the insurance industry knows such a task would be challenging to say the least. Nevertheless, the new director undertook it, and he and others gave it their best. Early on, it looked as if they might succeed. For example, in May 1967, it was reported to the Board that the agency department had produced over $90 million of new individual life coverage in the first three years of its existence. However, by 1969, the high costs incurred by marketing through an agency system began to become more and more apparent. That year, CUNA Mutual hired the actuarial consulting firm of Milliman and Robertson to study their individual life program. In January 1970, management reported to the board on the results of that study and made several recommendations. It was concluded that the following steps should be taken: (1) revise the policy structure, (2) eliminate unprofitable products, (3) explore mass marketing approaches, (4) closely monitor and limit surplus impact of individual life sales, and (5) work toward a new portfolio of products, ones better matched to the company's future marketing direction.

Energy and time were devoted to these and other steps during the first half of the 1970s, but by July 1976, board minutes indicate that "Agency operations have been held static for the last few years pending development of the Individual Marketing Program and the plan is not to add substantially to the agency staff until the new Individual Marketing plan is established."

The company continued to develop what it called Member Marketing through personal selling, direct mail, and credit union service centers, and by 1978, the agency force had been integrated into the Member Marketing Department. Concern continued, however, about the drain on surplus generated by member coverage and, in August of 1981, a company task force that had been looking into ways to deal with this issue delivered its report to the board. The report suggested "reorganization of the supervision of member coverage."

Acquisition of League Companies

In 1983, CUNA Mutual took another step which had several objectives, one of which was to enhance its individual insurance capabilities. In that year the company acquired the League Life and League General Insurance companies, both of which had been owned by the Michigan Credit Union League. In 1958, during a period of controversy concerning new CUNA Mutual programs, the Michigan league had acquired a life insurance company, which they named League Life, to provide its members an alternative to CUNA Mutual. In 1966, the league acquired a dormant property insurance company and named it League General. These two companies had succeeded, largely through direct mail, in achieving over a 50 percent share of the credit union business in Michigan. CUNA Mutual had tried valiantly to maintain its share of the Michigan market but, by 1982, that share had shrunk to about 25 percent. When the Michigan League ran into financial problems later that year, CUNA Mutual's president was able to work out an agreement with the League Companies' president that resulted in the sale of the companies to CUNA Mutual. CUNA Mutual's experience with the acquisition of the League Companies is an important precursor to its affiliation with Century Companies for a number of reasons. Perhaps most prominent is that CUNA Mutual's relationship with the League Companies remained problematic for several years. Part of the reason for this is that a history of competition had existed between them for some time and this was particularly salient among the field people. But another factor was the relationship of CUNA Mutual's senior management people with the man who had been the League Companies' president. For whatever reason there were feelings on his part that Madison was slowly imposing on his autonomy. At the same time, CUNA Mutual management was developing the feeling that Southfield, Michigan (where the League Companies were located), needed to be more fully integrated into the CUNA Mutual Group. The manager who was in charge of the Life division at League Life at the time recalls that, "It seemed to us like Madison didn't care how much money was wasted or how many people were hurt by their decisions, but, looking back, it was just that our management people in Southfield were not communicating to us in a timely way what it was that Madison wanted us to do." CUNA Mutual management learned a great deal from this experience and, as we will see later in our story, they put this learning to very good use in the early stages of their relationship with Century Companies.

National Liberty

The company's struggles with the challenges inherent in providing individual coverage continued and eventually management turned to consideration of some kind of joint venture with another company. In March of 1983, the executive committee of the board granted management the authority to proceed with negotiations with National Liberty Marketing, Inc. to market, through direct response, life, accident, and health products. According to CUNA Mutual's chief corporate staff officer who, along with the CEO, was actively involved in negotiating the deal with National Liberty, "This was a 50/50 ownership deal in which CUNA Mutual remained heavily involved not only in the ongoing management, but at the policy making level as well." Some concern was expressed by some members of management that the joint venture might create "inflexibility in managing CUNA Mutual's future approach to the individual life market," but CUNA Mutual was very interested in National Liberty's direct response expertise and so the venture went forward. It is interesting to note that when the final vote was taken by CUNA Mutual's Joint Administrative Committee on whether to go ahead with the National Liberty deal, the vote was two in favor (the CEO and the COO) and nine against. So, as one of the company officers told us, "The deal went ahead." When asked how a deal that had been voted down nine to two could go ahead, the same officer said, "Well, the CEO is still the CEO." The most vociferous objector to the deal was appointed by the CEO to oversee the implementation and management of the joint venture. CUNA Mutual's chief corporate staff officer recalls that some of the other objections to the National Liberty relationship came from people who thought the direct response expertise that National Liberty would contribute already existed in CUNA Mutual. For example, he recalls that the League Companies' president felt that his company's direct response knowledge was being underutilized and CUNA Mutual's internal direct response people also thought they had the required direct response capabilities. Nevertheless, this joint venture has worked very well for CUNA Mutual but, since it has been limited to the direct response marketing approach, it could not be expected to address some of their other needs in the individual marketing area, and, therefore, they have continued to try to address those needs.

Colonial Penn

CUNA Mutual also entered into a joint venture with Colonial Penn at about the same time. It was reported in our interviews that this was, "an automobile insurance deal in which we (CUNA Mutual) held only a 10 percent interest with Colonial Penn holding the other 90 percent." In spite of the fact that CUNA Mutual was, at first, very comfortable with the Colonial Penn people, several obstacles were encountered and eventually this arrangement was terminated, and, in the opinion of at least one CUNA Mutual Officer, "This was a good learning experience. We learned that we never again wanted to be part of a joint venture in which we did not maintain a high level of involvement both at the policy making and operational levels. We decided then that we could not afford to allow another company to come into our marketplace and do business without our intense involvement and oversight." As we shall see, this thinking has had a significant impact on CUNA Mutual's relationship with Century Companies.

International Financial Services

CUNA Mutual was receiving pressure from large credit unions to get into face-to-face selling. The large credit unions were in competition with other financial institutions to provide broader financial services to individual members. In the early 1980s, the State leagues, in an effort to support their membership, began to pressure CUNA Mutual to consider programs that would meet these needs. The large credit unions probably had the capacity to "go it alone" just like other large financial institutions in the country, but the leagues, in order to try to protect their domains and to take advantage of the potential critical mass in their states, joined in leading the effort to get individual insurance and annuity products to their membership. In turn, CUNA Mutual stepped up its efforts to find ways to offer such individual products. As part of this initiative, in November of 1984, the board authorized management to complete and execute an agreement with a company called International Financial Services (IFS). This arrangement was expected to afford CUNA Mutual consulting services, reinsurance and insurance products so that the company could enter the field of location sales of life insurance and financial services to members of credit unions. IFS was owned and headed by a man who had developed a franchise approach to marketing financial services which he called "Money Concepts" and who was headquartered in North Palm Beach, Florida. He had an excellent sales record in individual insurance and seemed to have a creative marketing approach, and so, by February of 1985, CUNA Mutual and IFS had worked out an arrangement by which the "Money Concepts" system could be used as a financial planning distribution system to credit unions. The plan was to arrange league sponsorship to sell franchises to credit unions for the distribution of insurance and credit union products and to arrange for the funding to launch the program to be provided by the credit unions themselves through this franchise arrangement. This program was named the "Plan America Credit Union Financial Planning Network," and later became referred to within the company as "Plan America I." There were, as one might expect, some start-up problems with the system, but all in all, it began rather well and a number of Plan America I franchises still operate today.

But that gets well ahead of our story, so let us go back to May 1986. In that month, the CUNA Mutual Board learned that the IFS head was interested in selling a percentage of IFS to CUNA Mutual. It was decided that an independent assessment of IFS should be performed before any recommendation was made. The head of CUNA Mutual's corporate staff group was asked to conduct this assessment, and he enlisted the help of the Duff and Phelps firm to complete the project. This assessment resulted in a decision, in December of 1986, not to purchase an interest in IFS, but to continue with the previous arrangement. However, in the interim, two important things had taken place. First, in September, CUNA Mutual had undertaken a study of how they should approach any future attempts at getting into the individual insurance business. This study was being conducted by three of CUNA Mutual's Officers, and it recommended that a merger would be the best alternative. A list of requirements that CUNA Mutual would impose in any arrangement with another company had evolved out of the experiences with Colonial Penn and National Liberty. This list, which became known internally as the "Eleven Commandments," was to have significant impact on CUNA Mutual's negotiations with Century Companies, and we will return to this issue later in this chapter. In addition, the study included a list of companies that the study group considered potential candidates for merger and Century was among those companies. Second, in November of 1986, the CUNA Mutual CEO had met the Century Companies CEO at an executive seminar held at Harvard University. This chance meeting was to have profound impacts on the futures of both of their companies, as well as CUNA Mutual's relationship with IFS.

The impact of these events on the two companies, CUNA Mutual and Century, was substantial, but, before we get to that, let us follow the IFS story to its conclusion. As noted above, CUNA Mutual decided not to purchase an interest in IFS and, in March 1988, Century Companies became the product provider and manager of Plan America. But once again, that gets us ahead of our story. Let us go back and recount Century's activities leading up to the affiliation.

CENTURY'S DRIVE TO ADAPT TO THE 1980s AND 1990s

As we described in Chapter 3, Century Companies had been, for most of its history, what might be called a typical mutual insurance company. It differed from CUNA Mutual in many respects, as we also have discussed in Chapter 3, and one of those differences was that Century had been an individual life company, whereas CUNA Mutual had been primarily a group company. As a relatively small individual life company, Century had been strongly affected by the industry conditions described in Chapter 4, and it was in an attempt to respond to those conditions that the company began to modify its culture in the late 1970s.

First Downsizing

Perhaps the first indicator that things were changing took place in April of 1979, when, for the first time in the company's history, they underwent a "downsizing." This consisted of a reduction of just eight people, but it sent a shockwave through the halls of Lutheran Mutual, as the company was then called. Company management was concerned enough with people's reaction that a psychological guru of the insurance industry, Ralph Hershowitz, was brought in to help handle the "culture shock." One of the company's senior managers recalls that, "Up until that time, Century was the place to be in our town, in that it was very secure. The downsizing knocked some reality into us that let us know we were subject to the same pressures as any other business, which is something we should have realized long before."

Board Marketing Committee and CLIC

In June 1980 the company established a marketing committee on the board of directors because of concern about the continuing problems with the volume of new business. Later in that year, the board spent considerable time discussing the general condition of the insurance industry and, in November, decided to authorize the formation of a stock subsidiary of the company called Century Life Insurance Company (CLIC). In August 1981, a management marketing committee reported that their study showed that the company needed to focus more clearly on certain markets, and steps were taken to move in that direction.

Broker/Dealer and CIMCO

By early 1982, it had become apparent that further steps would be necessary if the company was to compete successfully in the evolving market. In May of that year, the board voted to form a Broker/Dealer, to set up an investment company called Century Investment Management Company (CIMCO) and to establish a money market fund. The fact that Century had substantial professional investment expertise later became a factor in the affiliation with CUNA Mutual, and we will return to that issue in later chapters when we discuss the continuing integration of the companies.

Direct Recognition

As a reponse to the increasing tendency of policyowners to take advantage of the low interest rates on policy loans (see Chapter 4), the company began a "direct recognition" program in 1983. This meant that the company's practice of continuing to pay dividends on the full amount of the cash value in a policy even if it had been borrowed against would cease. Henceforth, the amount of any policy loans would be "recognized" in dividend payments.

Formation of the Project Steering Committee

All of this activity was necessitating a great deal of task force and special project activity in the company, and in 1983, it became obvious that some kind of control over the number and scope of these projects was necessary. The company formed a standing committee called the Project Steering Committee (PSC) to which all projects had to be submitted for scrutiny so that there could be a formal allocation of resources. This was a significant step because it went a long way toward creating the "process orientation" that later became so pervasive in the Century culture. One of Century's managers who was involved in the development of the company's project management discipline offered the opinion that Century would not have been able to succeed in the development and management of Plan America, the original joint venture with CUNA Mutual, if it had not had this project management capability. As we discussed in Chapter 4, this process orientation differed significantly from the more opportunistic approach to planning and decision making that was often followed in CUNA Mutual. This difference between the companies created some challenges, as we will see in later chapters, during the early work on Plan America, the due diligence process, and still later as the integration of the two companies progressed through such issues as allocation of financial resources, investment decisions, and personnel decisions.

Buying the Plane

In mid-1983 it was decided that the company needed an airplane to handle the greatly increased amount of executive travel, and in December of that year Century purchased a plane. CUNA Mutual's CEO later said that the fact that Century had a plane may have been crucial in facilitating his company's affiliation with the Iowa firm. He pointed out that both commercial air and automobile travel between Waverly, Iowa, and Madison, Wisconsin, are very inconvenient and the plane made it much easier to have the frequent meetings that were necessary to keep the extended negotiations moving ahead. He went so far as to say "Without the plane, this whole thing might never have taken place." The purchase of the plane, along with many of the changes described above, should give the reader the impression that Century was trying to do those things that would allow it to compete as a general financial services company in what was obviously a rapidly changing marketplace.

The Interstate Exploration

This struggle continued, and in 1984 the company first considered establishing a permanent relationship with another company: Interstate Insurance located in Des Moines, Iowa. Several Century management people were involved in gathering information about Interstate and one of them recalled that their investigation led them to conclude that Interstate was not a company in which they would be interested for two reasons. One was that its distribution system was entirely made up of brokerage, and the other was that, "It seemed like their executives did not have the focus on policyholders that prevailed at Century. However, the Century people found the experience an intriguing one and their interest in the possibility of some sort of relationship with another company was piqued. One of Century's few executives who had work experience in other companies that had gone through a merger, (he had worked for both Equitable of Iowa and for Connecticut General) particularly liked the idea that, "We were looking outside our four walls for opportunities."

The Name Change

In that same year a major step was taken when the company's 100-plus-year old identity was changed by giving up the Lutheran Mutual name and replacing it with the Century Companies name. The significance of this move should be apparent after reading about the company's history in Chapter 3, and it should be no surprise that many, including company staff members, policyholders, and members of the Waverly, Iowa, community were upset by this change.

Some 80,000 Century policyholders voted on the change and the approval passed by a significant margin, but the CEO asked the staff to give him the names of the two dozen policyholders who had been most vocally opposed to the name change. By far the majority of these were Lutheran pastors. The CEO then decided to make personal telephone calls to each of them to get a feeling for the reasons for their objection. As he recalls, the general tone was that they felt the company was "giving up on the church," and his response was to explain some of the background for the decision and to point out that over the years he had received calls from pastors who would typically complain that the company was "using the name of the church in the interest of securing business." It became clear that the company was not going to win this one in everyone's eyes.

However, some were very pleased by the change since they felt it opened new opportunities. The name change was much more than a symbolic move because even though the company had sold to non-Lutherans for some time, it constituted stepping out completely for the first time into a nonsponsored market, and, as such, it meant that the company was committing to try to "play with the big dogs," as one of the company's officers put it.

Asset/Liability Problems, Expense Increases, and UL/VUL

For several years company management had been concerned with the growing mismatch of the company's assets and liabilities, and in January of 1985 they moved to become more aggressive in matching by giving up some yield. Matching assets and liabilities had not been a prominent issue during the "comfort zone" prior to the 1980s, but when policyholders began to ask for their funds, it meant that companies either had to borrow money or sell their assets at a discount. Thus matching assets and liabilities became a new and crucial management consideration. In spite of Century management's efforts, company data showed that expenses had increased 15 percent between 1983 and 1985 and that, in spite of the fact that the company had managed to develop and was marketing some very state-of-the-art products such a Universal Life (UL) and even a Variable Universal Life (VUL) product, and had taken all of the steps described above, they had not managed to turn their situation around. It is important to note, however, that the company's product development achievements later became a significant factor in the affiliation. That is, as Century's ontroller commented, "the fact that we had developed a VUL product, and that it was one of the very first to be developed in the entire industry, was an important consideration to CUNA Mutual, since it clearly demonstrated our product development capability." These feelings were confirmed in interviews with several CUNA Mutual executives.

Distribution Cost Problems

Century's CEO recalls that during this time he and others began to see that the real problem was in the productivity and/or the expense per unit sold of the distribution system, and this was not affected by attempts, however successful, to reduce home office expenses. He also recalls that, when they realized that the key was to reduce distribution costs, they explored some options for doing so, such as putting agents in banks or savings and loan offices. Century's vice president of marketing at the time recalls these efforts and says, "We never had more than about a half dozen reps working this way at one time and it was very difficult to arrange." In fact, they concluded that the logistics, which required negotiating separate arrangements with each bank or S&L, were prohibitively complex. The marketing VP also remembers that he and the CEO, "discussed possible sponsored market opportunities such as some sort of arrangement with the American Bankers Association, (which we learned had just signed an agreement with a subsidiary of Mutual Life of Canada) and with the Credit Union Movement, which we knew was served by CUNA Mutual."

Surplus Study

In the first half of 1985, management formed a special task force to conduct what became known in the company as "The Surplus Study." This task force, consisting of three senior financial officers, worked fulltime for about one year to analyze the impact on surplus of a variety of company policies and practices. Many insurance companies have since undertaken similar studies, but this was one of the earliest comprehensive attempts to understand what is really a very complex business. The result was that, perhaps for the first time, management truly understood the implications of many of the variables involved in the management of a mutual insurance company, and, when they did, they realized that, if the company were to survive and prosper, some fundamental changes were going to be necessary.

As a result of this "surplus study," it became apparent that the company was going to have to grow substantially in order to achieve the necessary critical mass to compete, and this would, of course, require substantial funding. It may be worth noting here that not all of the company's executives agreed that continued growth was necessary. The company's chief financial officer (CFO), who had directed the surplus study became convinced that the investment required for continued growth could be made only by dipping into the returns to existing policyholders, and he was adamant that to do so was indefensible. The CEO argued that if the company just "hunkered down" to protect the investment of current policyholders, it could survive for a while but would ultimately become what he referred to as the "Moribund Mutual," and that this would, in the end, serve nobody, *including* the current policyholders. The CFO remained unconvinced and, in fact, voluntarily stepped down from his position as chief financial officer and ultimately (a couple of years later) left the company when the company decided to press on in its search for ways to finance its growth.

Further Downsizing

While studying the alternatives for funding that growth, the company decided that expenses needed to be reduced rapidly in the interim, and, in January of 1986, the second downsizing was undertaken. This one involved about thirty people, including some highly placed executives, and once again produced significant shock waves in the company and this time in the Waverly community as well. The CEO in particular went through a difficult period as a result of the reactions of colleagues and friends to this downsizing. To many, the decision to go ahead with this move was seen as his personal decision and one which demonstrated that the company was "not what it used to be." By implication then, *he* was not what he used to be, that is, a caring, compassionate person. He received phone calls and letters that were particularly vitriolic, and, in a community the size of Waverly (about 8,000 people), it was impossible to avoid being extremely visible.

By this time, Century had matured beyond being what it had historically been in a number of ways, only one of which was that company management had become much more sensitive to the issue of cost of operation. This led to yet another downsizing some months later which occurred during the time at which plans were being made for some of the public announcements concerning the affiliation with CUNA Mutual. This gets us ahead of our story and it involved only a few people, but we mention it here because it contributed substantially to the view of Century that eventually developed in CUNA Mutual. One of the people laid off at this time had been in charge of public relations for Century. He was not let go because of the quality of his performance, but rather because Century management had decided they needed to reduce staff by a few people in order to hit a particular projected budget figure, and that the best way to do it was to eliminate a few small functional areas. One of those areas turned out to be public relations. Looking back on it, a time when the company was undertaking a change as major as the affiliation was probably not the time to eliminate this particular function, but it was done. A member of CUNA Mutual's public relations staff remembers how he felt when he heard Century had let its public relations director go. "I thought it was awful," he says, "and I remember that one of my colleagues in public relations asked if I thought we were about to publicize our own demise." This view of Century as somehow preoccupied with cutting costs even if people were to be hurt became quite widespread in CUNA Mutual and, as we shall see later in our story, had some effect on the progress of the affiliation.

It may also be relevant to mention at this point that this particular event (that is, the layoff of the PR director and a few others) had a specific sort of effect within Century as well. Up until that point, even though there had already been some downsizing, it was pretty clear to Century associates that if you were performing your job well, you were safe from losing it. However, now *that* was not even a certainty. It now seemed that even if you *were* a good performer, you might be part of a reduction in force, and, for some Century people, this seemed to have something to do with the affiliation.

Consideration of Alternatives for Financing Growth

In September 1986, a management task force delivered a report to the executive officers which outlined the company's alternatives for financing its growth. After considering alternative funding sources including (1) internal ones such as reserve adjustments, sale/leaseback of home office real estate, and so on, (2) surplus reinsurance, and (3) various capitalization plans such as joint ventures, a public offering or an employee stock ownership plan, the report offered a number of recommendations and commmented on other methods of funding growth as follows: "The three methods discussed in this report are not the only alternatives to funding growth. Other possibilities, such as mergers, acquisitions, and affiliations may be equally or more attractive as a means of achieving our corporate growth plans. These alternatives have not been explored in this report. If there is any support for these or any other methods, information should be developed for consideration along with the ideas discussed here."

The Volunteer MBA Group

As it turned out, there *was* some support for some of these alternatives and some of it came from a "volunteer" group of middle-management people in the company, all of whom held or had been working on Masters of Business Administration (MBA) degrees at the University of Northern Iowa. This group had formed and met on their own time because they felt that the company lacked a clear, or at least a clearly communicated, corporate growth objective and strategy and because they desired to make a contribution to the same. One of them recalls that "we met at different times and places, sometimes on Saturday mornings at people's houses where we'd have coffee and discuss our ideas." Most of them had taken, during their MBA program, a course in which a model of corporate strategies developed by Harvard University professor Michael Porter had been presented, and they began to apply that model to their own company. They eventually delivered a report, called "Potential of a Business Affiliation Strategy in Achieving Long Term Objectives of Century Companies of America," to the executive officers on December 5, 1986. The last line of their report reads; "An affiliation strategy is manageable and can be used to help us reach our objective rapidly rather than incrementally."

The Century CEO remembers being particulary impressed by this group, not only because of the quality of the work they had done, but because "they had shown the interest and taken the initiative to do all of this on their own time. They were among our very best and brightest young managers, and I was inclined to take their ideas very seriously."

Some of the members of the MBA group were not sure how their presentation had been viewed by the company's executives. He recalls that they received little direct feedback except from the CEO who met subsequently with the group to express his appreciation. At this meeting, one group member recalled that the group presented the CEO, who was known to wear a headband during his daily workouts, with a new one which read "MERGER" and a T-shirt that read "It wasn't raining when Noah built the ark." (This was a quote from a talk that the CEO had heard at an insurance industry meeting and which he had subsequently used in addressing company management meetings. The MBA group was, therefore, using the CEOs own comment to signal him that they felt it was time to take steps to be prepared for coming changes in the insurance industry.)

It is probably true that this group's activities had much more impact on the company than they realized at the time. For example, in their report they used the word "affiliation" as an umbrella term to describe any of a number of different forms of relationship between two companies, from joint venture to complete merger, and this term was eventually adopted by the two companies to describe their relationship. In addition, as part of their report, the MBA group had presented a list of what they felt were the assets Century would bring to the table in any potential organizational combination and their list looked very similar in general content as well as specific wording to other documents developed later in the affiliation process. Finally, it is of interest to note that among the companies the group referred to in their report as examples of organizations that had found a particular market "niche" was one called CUNA Mutual.

It was during the period in which this group had been meeting and preparing their report that the Century CEO attended the seminar at Harvard University where he met CUNA Mutual's COO, (who later during the affiliation process, became the CEO.) The members of the group could not have known that the growth strategy they were advocating was in the very early exploration stages at that very moment.

PREAFFILIATION STEPS

The Harvard University Meeting

In November of 1986, IBM sponsored one in a series of seminars which they offered to their client companies. This one focused on the impact of social change on business and exploring strategic options for corporations, and it was attended by top executives from a number of different companies.

The CUNA Mutual CEO remembers that when he was entering the building at Harvard in which the seminar was to be held, the Century CEO happened to be arriving at precisely the same moment. He recalled that "we had actually met a couple of times before. The first time was during my time on the Board of the Lutheran Brotherhood when he (the Century CEO) had been a candidate for their CEO position. Later, we were reintroduced at an industry convention by a mutual friend. I had also heard lots of good things about him from others in the industry, particularly those at Lutheran Brotherhood since they often used Century as a comparison company."

The CUNA Mutual and Century leaders entered the seminar room together and took seats next to each other. A presentation by Professor Warren McFarlan on the topic of changes taking place in society led the two to have a wide-ranging discussion at lunch, during which they agreed that organizations that failed to plan for and take charge of their futures were unlikely to succeed.

It is important to keep in mind that at the time he attended this seminar, Century's CEO had been wrestling for some time with the problem of how to finance the growth he knew his company needed. He also had concluded that the most promising route to take was to form some sort of affiliation with another company, and he knew that the high costs associated with the standard method of distributing insurance products made it unattractive to affiliate with another typical mutual company operating in an unsponsored market.

For his part, the CUNA Mutual CEO recalled that during the seminar presentations, as well as during his informal discussions with Century's head, he was thinking about the facts that (1) his company had a market, but did not serve it as well as he wished they could, and (2) they had spent many years and many dollars trying to get into the individual life business without much success, and (3) as chief operating officer, he very much wanted to break that log-jam. It occurred to him that Century might offer some opportunities to do so, but he recalls that they did not discuss anything about a possible relationship at that time, even though the Century CEO did mention that, although his company was strong currently, he foresaw difficulties in the areas of asset/liability management and distribution costs. Century's leader recalls: "I think we had every breakfast and lunch together during the three-day meeting and we learned a lot about each other's companies and views. I was thinking about some of the possibilities that might exist if our companies were to develop some kind of relationship, but we didn't discuss it at that time."

As mentioned above, a CUNA Mutual study group had identified a number of companies they considered good potential merger candidates and Century was on that list. A CUNA Mutual executive recalls that shortly after his boss returned from the

Harvard seminar, during a meeting in which they were discussing this list, the boss told him that he found it interesting that Century was included on the list because he had just spent some time with their CEO. Later during that meeting, the CUNA Mutual leader called Century's CEO to tell him that some staff work had been done since they had met at Harvard and that he would like to meet again. Prior to the meeting at Harvard, the CUNA Mutual study group had recommended that their company explore a possible relationship with Maccabees Mutual Life as the first choice on the list, but as one of the study group says, "the fortuitous meeting between our leader and Century's moved Century to the top because it seemed like we might have not only an interesting, but an *interested*, potential partner." Evidently, the CUNA Mutual leader had concluded from his conversations with Century's CEO that there might be some mutual interest, even though there had been no *direct* discusssion of the topic. CUNA Mutual's chief corporate staff officer feels that the Century/CUNA Mutual affiliation may have eventually taken place even if the CEOs had not met at Harvard, but that it would certainly have taken place much later. And he said, "it might *never* have occurred if, in our explorations with other companies on the list, we had found another willing partner before contacting Century."

The ACLI Meeting in San Francisco

The next opportunity for the two CEOs to meet came at an American College of Life Insurance (ACLI) meeting which took place in San Francisco in November 1986. During the ACLI meeting, which lasted several days, they found time to meet "two or three times," according to their best recollections. Two other CUNA Mutual executives who were also attending the ACLI meeting, sat in on these discussions. One of them, the chief legal officer, recalls feeling that "[the Century CEO] seemed to me to be someone with whom it would be very pleasant to have a business relationship and it seemed we had something to offer each other. I recall quite clearly that I felt much better about him than I had about the head of IFS." CUNA Mutual's chief corporate staff officer recalls that "[the Century CEO] required that we meet outside the hotel where the ACLI was meeting and I presume this was to avoid alerting, or perhaps alarming, his people. I found this a bit amusing at first, but I could also understand his caution since CUNA Mutual's approach at the time was to achieve a merger with us as the survivor and I am sure that he was interested in some kind of joint venture. He also had a relatively young senior staff who might bolt if they thought he was up to something they didn't like." CUNA Mutual's head of government relations was also attending the ACLI meeting and he recalls that his executives seemed to be, "off doing something a lot of the time, and I found out what it was on the last day of the meeting when our COO told me about their discussions with Century and swore me to silence."

The discussions in San Francisco produced substantial interest in both parties and, as a result, there were internal discussions in both companies. The Century CEO recalls that he "tested the waters" with some of his senior management by asking how they would feel about some kind of joint venture which involved marketing their products through a larger institution. He remembers that, "our CFO asked what kind of institution I meant and when I said, 'Credit unions,' he said, 'You are talking about CUNA Mutual,' so that was the first time any of us talked about them by name." He also recalls that most of his senior people seemed generally positive about the possibility of some kind of joint venture, but he remained reluctant to involve them too deeply because he knew that CUNA Mutual's agenda was not exactly the same as his at that point.

The extent to which the Century CEO felt he could divulge to his people the nature of the discussions he was having with CUNA Mutual eventually became one of the most important issues in our story. It, therefore, deserves some explanation at this point.

The CEOs Dilemma: What to Tell to Whom and When to Tell It

This aspect of our story holds a great deal of interest for both authors and, we hope will do the same for the reader.   One of the most difficult issues for executives involved in major change in their organizations is that of deciding to what extent, and when, to pass on information to their people.   One sometimes reads or hears the recommendation "Tell all you can as soon as you can," but we hope to show that such advice assumes a clarity that is seldom, if ever, the case in the complex world of major organizational change. To begin with, it is important to remember that the Century CEO had become absolutely convinced that his company had to undertake a major change in order to have a viable future, and that the studies he and his senior managers had already completed had led him to the conclusion that some sort of relationship with another company was the only really promising route to follow. Now add to those facts the idea that it was also clear to him that to involve his company with another "standard" mutual company was not the answer because any such company would have the same high distribution costs that Century had. This meant that he needed to find a company that was operating in some sort of institutionally sponsored market. It should be obvious that the list of such organizations would be very short indeed, and yet, here he was in a position to establish a relationship with exactly that sort of organization! However, there was one major problem, and it was that this organization had a different idea than he did, and certainly different than his people did, of the form that such a relationship should take. At a general level, he had perceived that CUNA Mutual's interest was in a merger with themselves (CUNA Mutual Insurance Group or CMIG) as survivor and he knew that neither he nor his people would be interested in that kind of arrangement. It later became apparent that this issue would not be a problem, but he had no way of knowing that at the time.

More specific, and more troublesome over the long term, were the requirements that CUNA Mutual had developed for *any* sort of relationship with another company. This list, which we referred to earlier as the "Eleven Commandments," included such items as the following:

- All products must bear a CMIG label, or the label of another provider should be kept as inconspicuous as possible.
- All contact with credit unions is to be by CMIG representatives. All contact with members is to be approved by CMIG. All marketing materials are to be subjected to CMIG review

procedures.
- Analysis of the long-term (minimum of five years) business impact and the results for CMIG should be made before final structuring of any arrangement.
- In the case of termination of the joint business venture, provision must be made for CMIG to become owners of the business or to somehow control future placement of it.

It should be apparent that these requirements were aimed at allowing CUNA Mutual to ensure that it would retain control of its marketplace. These ideas were not based on some hypothetical potential problems, but on CUNA Mutual's prior experience with joint ventures. Nevertheless, they presented a significant problem to Century's CEO, because he was in the position of being virtually certain that his company should proceed to develop some sort of relationship with CUNA Mutual but also of needing to keep CUNA Mutual's stringent requirements from frightening his people. He was confident that, given time, he would be able to engineer an agreement that would satisfy all parties. However, the key phrase here is "given time." He desperately needed to find a way to buy that time. He, therefore, undertook a strategy which was very much unlike his usual way of working with his people. It involved conducting discussions with CUNA Mutual on two levels simultaneously. One level (in which a number of Century people *were* involved) concerned the nature of the joint marketing venture, called Plan America II. The other level, in which for some time only the CEO and his board were involved, focused on the much bigger issue of a possible permanent affiliation of the two companies.

As the discussions proceeded and it became clear to Century's CEO that, among other requirements, CUNA Mutual was going to demand a majority position on the Century board, temporary confidentiality remained a necessity. CUNA Mutual's chief legal counsel recalls, "We knew that the Century CEO was not disclosing as much to his people as was being shared at CUNA Mutual, particularly on the issue of board control, and we were concerned about that, but we recognized that he was trying to control possible anxiety and that it was a lot easier for us to let people know what was going on since we were going to have board control. He, of course, could not reassure his people in that way, so he really had no choice at that point other than to say very little." CUNA Mutual's chief counsel expressed great admiration for the Century CEO's stance and comportment during this period. He commented, "It is very unusual to find a chief executive who has the long-range vision to see that the future of his company is such that they are going to have a difficult time going it alone *and* is willing to allow his company and himself to relinquish a substantial amount of control to establish a relationship which will allow them to survive and even prosper. I would describe his behavior as statesmanlike."

The extent to which the Century leader maintained the separation of the two levels of discussion is clear, in retrospect, from the comments of the man who was Century's chief legal counsel during the affiliation negotiations, who recalled that in December 1986, "shortly after our CEO met CUNA Mutual's COO, he told me that he wanted to talk with me about something he had cooking with a company called CUNA Mutual. He said he was working on something that might have legal implications and that it might be of mutual benefit to talk with some of their people since we may try to do some things together." However, the attorney remembers that he heard no more until March of that year when the CEO told him that "CUNA Mutual's chief legal counsel is working on something that involves us and you might need to be involved." Once again, the Century legal counsel heard no more about it, "except a couple of times during executive committee meetings of the board, which I attended because I was secretary of the corporation, and it was not even discussed much in those meetings." He remembers that, during this period, the board sometimes met in "executive session," but that he was not invited to attend those sessions. On some occasions, he recalled, "[our CEO] gave me brief summaries of those sessions to include in the minutes, but often he didn't even do that." In any event, it became apparent to the Century legal counsel, just as we indicated above, that there were two distinct levels of discussion going on between CUNA Mutual and Century and that neither he, nor any of the other Century staff except the CEO, were involved in both of those levels.

Normally the Century CEO shared a great deal of information with his people, and this more guarded approach was very uncomfortable for him and it led to some trying times. An example of the difficulty this strategy created is that Century's chief investment officer, (CIO), who later assumed the same position for the affiliated companies, recalls that "very early on I began to feel uncomfortable about the relationship with CUNA Mutual because our CEO often seemed to be hinting that maybe we should consider other ways of working together in addition to the joint marketing venture, but he also seemed to be holding back on us about exactly why he felt that way. That bothered me because he was never one to have hidden agendas and I sensed a hidden agenda here."

A similar perspective was offered by Century's chief financial officer at that time, who later became chief operating officer of Century and, still later, became operations head of entire Individual Life and Health division for the affiliated group. He had first heard about the possibility of some sort of relationship with CUNA Mutual shortly after the two CEOs had met in San Francisco. The Century CEO had described his discussions there to his executive officer (EO) group at the time and the (then) CFO recalls that "it is kind of funny now to realize how naive we were then. We thought this was just a new way to sell insurance. I remember that we (the EOs) went with our boss to Madison for a meeting in early 1987. The substance of the meeting was a presentation by the CUNA Mutual people on Plan America and what they were doing at that time (with IFS). He told us it was to be a secret meeting. That is, we were not to discuss it with anyone in Waverly." The CFO also remembers that it became pretty obvious that his boss considered this a very special issue when he suggested, after the meeting, that in spite of the Century policy that said that not more than two of the four top executives of the company were to fly on the company plane at once, he decided that it would be good if they all flew back to Iowa together so they could discuss their reactions immediately. The CFO also recalled a growing uneasiness on his part that, for a long time, meetings between his boss and CUNA Mutual people took place in Madison and even meetings involving several Century people also took place there. He remembers that his boss remained "very secretive" during this period and he began to feel that "maybe this was not an equal partners deal." He recalls asking his CEO why they did not have any meetings in Waverly and being told that it was important that they, "remain flexible. Maybe next time, they'll come here." "They didn't," he recalls. So, like the chief investment officer, the CFO began to feel uneasy, but, he says, "I still did not realize that we were embarking on a journey that would ultimately change Century so dramatically."

He does remember a particular EO meeting that took place in the spring of 1987 in which the CIO told the boss that he was sure there was more going on than was being shared and that he resented it and wanted to be brought up to date. The CFO says that their boss agreed he had not done a good job of "keeping the EOs in the loop," and he then proceeded to give them an update on the discussions he had been having with CUNA Mutual. However, as he remembers it, "That meeting was followed by another period of several months in which our leader conducted his shuttle talks in secret." It is the CFO's opinion that his boss was withholding information at that point, "because he knew that some of the possibilities would involve significant changes for some of our people such as geographical moves, job and reporting changes and, since he did not know whether such events would ever take place, he felt he did not need to disrupt people's lives at that point by talking about such things." The CFO says he is not sure he would have handled it any differently if he had been in the CEO's place.

It is clear in retrospect that the Century CEO's concern extended to, and was perhaps even most focused on, the members of the Century career agency system. Relationships with some of the members of this group were strained in general, and he knew that they might be very concerned and upset if they sensed that their company was considering a strategy that would result in a major change in market emphasis. However, he also felt strongly that the Plan America joint venture would demonstrate to the career system people the advantages of operating in a sponsored market. The reader should remember that the Century CEO had determined that a major problem his company faced was the unit costs involved in its distribution system, and this, he knew, meant that there would have to be substantial changes in that system. He anticipated, therefore, that he would get some resistance from members of that system. To minimize that resistance, he and other members of his management group presented the potential opportunity offered by the joint venture with CUNA Mutual in a very optimistic light to the members of their career system. The problems this caused will be explained fully in later chapters.

One more difficulty that the Century CEO faced should be mentioned here. He also had to educate his board concerning the changes that were occurring in the insurance industry so that they would be aware of the seriousness of the challenges faced by Century. He knew that he needed to have his board appreciate the company's situation in order for them to be willing to consider the major step of forming an affiliation with the much larger CUNA Mutual Insurance Group. He had been working on helping his board to become educated in this way for some time, but it was time to intensify his efforts in this regard. Shortly, we will discuss the steps involved in this process.

The CUNA Mutual CEO's Challenges

The situation, with respect to the management of information, was quite different for CUNA Mutual's COO (later CEO). For one thing, the whole issue of a possible relationship with another company was much less significant in CUNA Mutual than it was within Century. After all, it was something that had been undertaken before (with the League Companies and others), so this was just one more in a series of explorations. For another, it involved an individual life company, and most of the employees of CUNA Mutual were involved in the group part of the business and, therefore, would not be directly affected. Finally, even among those directly concerned, it was known that CUNA Mutual's interest was in a merger with itself as survivor, so the view was that the discussions were with, "some company we might buy." (The problems this eventually created as members of the two companies began to spend time together will be described in later chapters.)

This is not to imply that the CUNA Mutual leader faced no challenges in getting his company to move ahead with the discussions with Century. Prior joint ventures had always resulted in CUNA Mutual taking on additional work for employees in Madison. Furthermore, Plan America had been viewed as an opportunity for additional jobs in Madison. At the board of directors level it had been discussed and it was always assumed that any joint venture would, in fact, be a merger, which meant that to work through the idea of an affiliation with the board would make it appear that the CEO was backpedaling. He recalled that, "for some time, there were only three or four other people in CUNA Mutual who were really up to date on the status of our discussions with Century." One factor that affected his strategy at the beginning of these discussions was that he was not even the CEO of his company. He was COO and reported to the CEO, but he became the CEO in October of 1988. The prior CEO had been at the helm of CUNA Mutual for a period of fifteen years and was a much respected and loved leader in the company. He had given the COO a great deal of latitude which the COO had used to broaden the company's vistas by embarking on many of the steps described earlier in this chapter. In addition, the COO faced significant concern among some of his management people and, even more formidably, among some members of his board of directors, about the protection of CUNA Mutual's marketplace, the credit unions.

It would be difficult to overestimate the amount of concern that CUNA Mutual, as an organization, has about the protection of its marketplace. Many within the organization and on the board consider the company's relationship with the credit union movement to be the single most valuable asset the company has. This belief has led CUNA Mutual to guard very jealously that relationship and to be extremely reluctant to allow anyone access to that marketplace. What the COO was proposing, that is to form a long-term relationship with an individual life company that had several hundred sales representatives, seemed to some to be a very high-risk strategy. To help clarify this point, it may be important to explain that CUNA Mutual has always had a unique relationship with its board in that the board is made up primarily of credit union people. In this sense the board *is* the marketplace! CUNA Mutual is, in a sense, a creation of its market, and its charter very clearly reflects this fact. The charter makes it explicit that the company exists to serve the credit union movement and that it is obligated to focus its marketing efforts *entirely* on the credit unions and their members. Some members of the company and the Board, therefore, were concerned that it might be difficult to control the marketing efforts of the many sales representatives that were associated with Century.

Another issue of interest here (and one to which we shall return in a later chapter) is that of the management styles of the key players in our story. The Century CEO's style of leading was, in some senses, a combination of those of CUNA Mutual's CEO and COO. As we have noted, CUNA Mutual's CEO was a widely admired leader at his company as was the Century CEO at his company. The similarity between the two was probably what accounted for the Century CEO's almost immediate acceptance, later on, by many of the CUNA Mutual people. Both were very warm, caring, people-oriented leaders. During the extended affiliation process CUNA Mutual was going through the CEO transition and, as is common when there is change at the top, some CUNA Mutual people may not have been as comfortable with their new CEO's more market-driven, visionary style as they had been with his predecessor. However, it is also true that the former CUNA Mutual CEO was probably more conservative and internally focused than he was a market visionary. In that sense, the new CEO was the right man for the time at CUNA Mutual. He was visionary not only about the future of the market but about the structure and form of his company as well. The Century CEO was also a market visionary, and it was this shared orientation that initially drew the two leaders together at Harvard. As they listened to the seminar presentations they reacted similarly. Though their management styles may have been different, the driving force in their relationship was that they both could see the merits in bringing the two companies together to build a sustainable future that would make both companies stronger.

On this subject, the CUNA Mutual CEO's opinion is that "it is probably true that, regardless of the fit between our two companies, if Century's CEO and I had been two different people, this affiliation would probably never have taken place. It is the chemistry between people, whether they have common vision, values and goals, and whether they are committed to their organizations that determines whether there will be a lasting relationship. After talking with him at Harvard, I felt that he was a CEO who wanted to do what was best for his company and that he was not a person who was likely to let his ego get in the way in that he would be able to put his personal needs and desires aside in a search for a good agreement."

The Discussions Move Ahead

In spite of the respective challenges faced by both leaders, each succeeded in having his company move ahead with discussions. In January of 1987, the Century board had its first extended discussion concerning the possibility of a permanent affiliation with CUNA Mutual. One of the Century managers recalls that, at about that time, "(our CEO) asked me to do some research on a company called CUNA Mutual Insurance. He told me they needed a profile of the company, including a description of their organizational structure, their financials, their subsidiaries, etc." This information was later used as a basis for the board meeting, and it was shared with Century's EOs prior to their first meeting with CUNA Mutual, which would take place in the early spring of 1987. CUNA Mutual had already done some homework on Century Companies and they continued to amass further information. In January 1987 the CUNA Mutual board voted to authorize management to "continue pursuit of a merger with Century Companies." In February the Century board formed an ad hoc committee to work with their CEO on the potential relationship with CUNA Mutual, and in that same month, the Century CEO addressed the CUNA Mutual board regarding Century Companies and the possible joint venture.

In addition, the two companies formed a joint project staff team to develop a business plan for the joint venture. One of the Century team members recalls that, "CUNA Mutual already had a kind of embryonic thing going but we didn't necessarily want to just duplicate that." In fact, they did *not* duplicate the kind of arrangement that CUNA Mutual had begun with IFS. As we mentioned earlier, what was finally worked out was *very* different, especially as regards funding and control. As the reader may remember, the system with IFS (later referred to as Plan America I) involved a franchise arrangement in which a credit union signed up as the franchisee and underwrote the start-up costs. In the arrangement worked out between CUNA Mutual and Century, referred to as Plan America II, there is no franchise. The credit union signs up to have one or more Plan America representatives work with its members and the start-up and training costs are borne by the affiliated group.

Even as the group began its work, it was evident that both companies still had their pockets of resistance. We will see how some of them became problems when we describe, in the following chapters, the nature of the joint venture, as well as the early experiences with developing it and making it work.

The Boards Approve the Joint Venture Business Plan

The business plan was finalized and presented to and approved by the Century board in July 1987. The plan called for a two year pilot involving "the development of face-to-face marketing of high quality, high benefit return life insurance, health insurance and equity products for credit union members involving up to eight sales production units in a maximum of four to seven states by the end of 1989," with a projected cost of about $2.5 million to each of the two companies. The Century board also got its first chance to meet the CUNA Mutual COO at this meeting. One of the Century managers who had worked on the plan and who was one of those who made the presentation to the board recalls that "it was evident that the wheels were very much in motion. Our plan was basically a good one but it would have been possible to shoot some rather large holes in it. When the board didn't do that, I concluded that they were not interested in a very tight financial case being made but rather were taking a broader, more long-term view of this venture." At this point this manager had no way of knowing exactly how right he was. That is, the board really *was* taking a broader view as we have already explained.

In May, CUNA Mutual's board had asked the Century CEO to function as a special liasion to facilitate discussions between his company and theirs. In addition, the

CUNA Mutual board had created an ad hoc Century Joint Venture committee. In July the CUNA Mutual board voted to adopt a Statement of Intent to enter into a business relationship with Century and, subsequent to adoption of that statement, the CUNA Mutual board also approved the joint venture business plan.

Once the boards had approved the business plan for the joint venture, the companies formed a joint staff team to develop a Partnership Agreement and to shape the details of the venture. This was a very labor intensive task requiring several months of work.

First Joint Board Meeting

In October 1987 the implementation plan developed by the joint staff team was presented to the first joint meeting between the boards of directors of the two companies. This meeting,, (held in New Orleans during the annual meeting of the Credit Union National Association so that the Century Board could be introduced to the culture of the credit union movement) was a special meeting of the boards called specifically to discuss the relationship between the two companies. It was a significant event in the development of the relationship between the two companies because, for many of the members of each of the boards, it was the very first time they had been afforded an opportunity to meet and begin to develop an understanding of their counterparts. Items on the agenda included the background and purposes of the joint venture, the updated business plan, and the long-term plans for the venture. After meeting together, the boards split up for private discussions and, after considering the implications of the step they were taking, the boards adopted a "statement of intent." This was not a legally binding document but it did indicate the sincere intent of the two companies to form a *permanent* relationship. This was crucial from the point of view of CUNA Mutual. As the reader will recall, CUNA Mutual was very concerned with the issue of protecting its market and this statement was designed to give them some reassurance that Century was not entering into the joint venture with the goal of getting a foothold in the credit union marketplace and then withdrawing from the joint venture while continuing to operate in the market. Several of the CUNA Mutual officers have said that, without the signing of this statement of intent, the relationship with Century would definitely not have gone forward. However, once it *was* signed, there was clearly a high level of trust on both sides and, two months later, in December, the managements and ad hoc board committees of both companies signed the Plan America Partnership Agreement.

In Chapter 6 we will follow our story on both of the two levels of progress that were now underway. That is, we will describe the development of the Plan America joint venture and we will detail the extensive due diligence process that was going on at the same time to prepare for the permanent affiliation of the two companies.

6

Evolution of the Affiliation

The Century CEO often said one thing that took more time than he had originally estimated was the number of times he had to explain not only the reason for the affiliation but the process. This is understandable because of the change in peoples' lives and because the affiliation itself was a new concept. You could not pick up a book and read about the process. Part of the reason for that confusion was that the companies chose to "design/build" the affiliation. The process of design/build will be explained in this chapter, but if the concept was confusing to those who were implementing the affiliation it probably will be confusing to the reader as well.

Chapters 1 through 5 took the reader through an historical sequence but the reader will find, because of this design/build concept, some overlapping with Chapters 6 and 7. We have allowed this repetition to remain to provide a clearer picture of what has occurred. In Chapter 6 we will review some broad phases of the affiliation, that is "building" the affiliation, from the initial contact between the boards and the staff to the point where the affiliation concept had been approved by all of the necessary constituencies and in effect was considered final. In Chapter 7 we will go back and explain some of the "design" concepts for the various phases of the affiliation.

INITIAL BOARD AND STAFF INTERACTION

As indicated in Chapter 5, it became apparent to the two executives in their meeting at Harvard that the potential synergy in a joint effort would support each company's attempt to build a sustainable strategy. The second meeting of the two was held a few weeks later in San Francisco at the American College of Life Insurance (ACLI) meeting as discussed in Chapter 5. This was a luncheon meeting where the purpose was to get to know each company better. It was apparent by the fact that the CUNA Mutual chief operating officer (COO) had two of his senior officers with him that the first meeting of the two leaders had been more openly discussed at CUNA Mutual than at Century.

After the discussion in San Francisco the Century chief executive officer (CEO) met with the Century board at the regularly scheduled November 1986 meeting to discuss his two conversations with the CUNA Mutual COO and indicated that he intended to involve the Century senior staff in the next meeting. At this point the intent was to focus on some type of joint distribution effort between the two companies.

It is significant to note that the topic of a joint marketing effort was discussed under the agenda item "organizational renewal" at the Century board meeting. For several years the Century CEO had felt that insurance companies were going to have to make some significant changes in their strategies if they were going to build sustainable futures. The item "organizational renewal" always appeared at the end of the agenda and was held in executive session with only the CEO and the board present. Sensitive items such as staffing changes, staff reductions, and other major concerns of the CEO were discussed in these sessions. The minutes for this particular item were always very general because it was felt that this would make it easier to implement any significant changes in the organization.

Shortly after the Board meeting the four senior officers of Century flew to Madison, Wisconsin to discuss the possibilities of a joint marketing effort. Century subsequently proposed a joint arrangement in the marketplace but it quickly became apparent that CUNA Mutual was not interested in bringing Century into their marketplace unless they could be assured that Century would not subsequently "go-it-alone." After a period of several months of developing a strategy, writing a business plan, adding a noncompetitive clause to the marketing arrangement, setting out detailed financials, committing human resources, and continually updating board members on progress, the Plan America concept was ready to be launched.

But before we move ahead to the initiation of the Plan America distribution system, it is instructive to reflect on cultural differences as perceived through those initial visits. Both staffs commented on the fact that the respective groups were friendly and professional but that the Century staff had a much narrower focus. It seemed as if each Century staff member was working on one project (the joint venture) compared to perhaps four or five for each CUNA Mutual person. CUNA Mutual staff had the feeling that this project was less important to them than it seemed to be to Century. The CUNA Mutual staff felt that they had not been told of the significance of this project, and to some it seemed that it was "sucking up" too many of their resources for simply being another of their many projects. Later on, to at least some of the CUNA Mutual staff, it became apparent that this project was their most important project.

PLAN AMERICA DISTRIBUTION SYSTEM INITIATED

As indicated earlier, the driving force for the affiliation was to address the distribution problems in the insurance business. To build a sustainable future the companies had to find a way to improve productivity in the distribution system and to lower the cost of distribution. The Plan America distribution system addressed these two fundamental problems.

At the outset the companies decided to split the startup costs for pilot operation and established a senior staff and board oversight committee. In addition a five person joint operational staff worked daily with the details of the business plan. Pilot operations were established in the states of Pennsylvania and Ohio. Both states had a significant concentration of credit unions and areas were picked in each state where Century did not have a heavy concentration of career agents. It was intended that the pilot operations would last two years before an evaluation would be made as to whether the venture should continue.

Since Century had the expertise in face-to-face selling, and because of the significance of this venture to both companies, Century assigned their chief marketing officer (CMO) to direct the project for both companies. As indicated above, many CUNA Mutual people were involved in a lot of projects and many on their staff did not appreciate the impact that this venture would have on CUNA Mutual in the long term. In addition, it should be recognized that this project impacted a relatively small portion of the CUNA Mutual business. In any event, when the Century CMO moved to Madison to carry on this assignment, he found that the contacts that he had before had been reassigned. In addition, he had neither a Secretary nor an assigned space. In fact, initially, it was not clear to whom he reported. While everyone was supportive, he in effect started a scratch operation in an environment and culture with which he was not familiar. From the point of view of the CUNA Mutual staff, the assignment of one of their actuaries to the project enhanced the communications process because they could better relate to the financials and the legitimacy of the venture. This move helped bring the importance of this venture into sharper focus for the CUNA Mutual staff.

One of the first steps Century took was to assign a middle- management officer full time in Waverly to the project. He was responsible for following up on some details of the project to try to assure that the companies were reaching their objectives. His early impressions were that there was a lot of excitement on the part of both CUNA Mutual and Century employees who were on the project team for the potential of the project but probably the most difficult thing in working with the two companies was establishing trust. Initial impressions were positive, but there were personality conflicts surfaced later as a result of finger-pointing by a few individuals in each company. However, there were enough individuals with cool heads who understood the objective and the potential of the joint venture, and these people ultimately prevailed. Through these struggles some strong relationships were formed which helped to feed and continue the process. To those who were working on the project it became obvious within a matter of months that it was going to be successful, that the pilot operation would be short lived and that some type of permanent relationship should be established.

Century also moved some of their second-line career managers into the pilot operations as district managers of representatives in the various credit unions. In addition, some Century agents were placed in key credit unions, but for the most part representatives in the credit unions were new recruits and agents from other companies. At the same time, CUNA Mutual assigned an individual from their marketing staff to act as a recruiter of credit unions and Century communicated to their office staff and field force the nature of the experiment and why it was necessary. Because the home office staff at Century had been focusing on the issue of productivity within the office it was easier for them to understand the necessity of the pilot program. For the Century field force it wasn't as easy. The field force was more dispersed and thus it was more difficult to address individual concerns and of course the diversion of management to another distribution system was threatening.

BOARD AD HOC COMMITTEE ESTABLISHED

The Century CEO knew that his company was dealing with more than just a marketing agreement and that it would not only be helpful but essential that the board of directors be involved on a continuous basis as opposed to waiting for regularly scheduled meetings. The Century board formed an ad hoc committee to oversee the progress of the relationship with CUNA Mutual. The committee consisted of three members of the board who had been involved in significant changes within their own companies plus the board chairman, who served as an ex officio member.

The CUNA Mutual CEO felt that they needed a permanent solution to their inability to tap face-to-face selling in their own market. He was also interested in more than just a marketing agreement. Therefore, to be consistent with the Century action the CUNA Mutual Board at the same time named an ad hoc committee similar to Century to meet with their CEO on an "as needed basis."

These committees met periodically as dictated by the progress that was being made in discussions between the two CEOs. These committees, for example, established A joint board marketing committee as mentioned in the previous section.

The CUNA Mutual board was probably further along in their understanding of the need for a permanent relationship of some kind between the two companies. However, they had always talked among themselves in terms of a merger, and because that was not the eventual direction the companies took, it did cause concern for some of the directors, sensing that management was leading them down a different path. There were a few CUNA Mutual board meetings where the ad hoc committee tried to update the entire board on the progress the two companies were making and some board members were extremely reluctant to proceed.

For the Century board, changes would be more traumatic and thus the effective utilization of the ad hoc committee was essential in maintaining a board/management partnership. For approximately two years the board and management had been having extensive discussions on the financial stress that the industry was facing and what that would mean to Century ten or fifteen years into the future. While the industry was experiencing a decrease in surplus (see Chapter 4) Century was determined to preserve its financial underpinnings. It was obvious that CUNA Mutual had the market and, therefore, Century would have to undergo the greatest change if they were serious about preserving their financial underpinnings in the long term and building a sustainable future.

When it became apparent that, not only was there extensive potential in the market to build a sustainable future but by moving some blocks of business to Waverly,

Century could improve its productivity and further strengthen its financial underpinnings immediately, the ad hoc committee began meeting approximately every two months.   At regularly scheduled board meetings there was always extensive discussion on the merits of the two companies continuing to work together. If a board member missed a meeting, the ad hoc committee made every effort to update that particular member. For example, the chairman and the CEO met in Chicago with one member to give a personal update on the discussions. A member of the ad hoc committee was flown to Madison for a personal review of the CUNA Mutual situation when he had missed a previous meeting. Retired directors from the Century board were invited to a special update meeting in Washington, D.C. to keep them apprised of the discussions. It was important to provide an opportunity for understanding for all those directors who had provided, and were continuing to provide, leadership for Century.

The ad hoc committees of the two boards met jointly as the discussions progressed. At one of the early meetings the Century chairman had misunderstood the time the meeting was to start and was late by one hour. At first the Cuna Mutual ad hoc members thought this was a ploy and that the chairman was taking the hard nosed approach to the discussions. This created some tension in the meeting but it was dealt with by openly discussing the misunderstanding. It quickly became apparent that all of the committee members from both companies were very anxious to work together for a common objective. Each of the CEOs also visited and periodically made a report to the other company's board. The ad hoc committees also arranged for the entire boards to meet in a joint session on several occasions.

These meetings were not without some tension. To try to depoliticize the sessions, each of the committees retained outside consultants to apprise them of issues of concern. More will be discussed in a later section on this issue. The committees held executive sessions without the CEOs in order to eliminate any personal agendas. The dominant emphasis of all of these discussions was to keep communications open and a focus on a strategy that would benefit the individuals that the board and management represented, that is the policyholders.

DEVELOPMENT OF THE PLAN AMERICA DISTRIBUTION SYSTEM

The original Plan America pilot program had been designed for two years. Some considerations emerged during the first year that caused progress to be inconsistent with the original business plan. First of all, CUNA Mutual did not "own" the credit unions. This, of course, had been understood by CUNA Mutual but not by Century. CUNA Mutual was the major provider for all credit union products and services and credit unions were their only market. Credit unions, of course, had other options making, in one sense, CUNA Mutual captive to the credit unions. Other factors were involved as well, but the net result was that it was proving more difficult to recruit credit unions into the plan than had been expected. Furthermore it was difficult to attract personnel to the new program and, once they were in place, to retain them. The intent was to deal with negative issues promptly and to build the plan on a series of successes. While there were some signs of success, these were not generally apparent to the credit unions throughout the area where the pilot program was being conducted.

Furthermore there was a tendency to write more securities than life insurance in credit unions. This meant that, to start with, the program results tended to be more "transaction" driven than "needs" driven. It is understandable why this would happen because some credit unions were looking for more activity and wanted quicker turnaround in transactions which would lead to an improved "bottom line." However, a "transaction" driven operation, while in the short term more profitable, was not what was called for in the business plan, which was focused on a sustainable future built on the "needs" selling approach. It was obvious that it was going to take longer than originally conceived.

When the CMO from Century moved to Madison to run Plan America, a newly appointed head of the career agency system in Waverly began reporting to the COO in Waverly. That created some uneasiness on the part of some members of the career system because as one field manager put it, "we lost our leader." The dilemma was that to have the new career marketing head in Waverly report to the CMO who had moved to Madison would dilute the CMO's effort on a project that was vital to the future of Century. At the same time it would create some confusion on the part of the Century career system at a time when career systems, in general, in the United States had been struggling. The Century CEO decided it was essential to keep the CMO focused on the success of Plan America. To add to the tension, the new career marketing head in Waverly did not relate well to the Century COO, partly because the COO was very financially oriented and, while the career marketing head was knowledgeable, he had had a previous experience with another company where there was evidence that he had run a "high cost" marketing staff. It also became apparent that the new marketing head for the career operation was having difficulty in buying into the concept of the Plan America operation. In field trips he began "knocking" what the company was trying to do, indicating that it was not achieving the needed results. The CEO and COO of Century repeatedly visited with him but reports of his negative conversations to field managers continued to filter back to the home office. During that period there were examples in the industry of other companies who were trying to make some radical changes where the field managers had successfully opposed the company changes to the point where it either caused a "run" on the company or the companies had to abort their plans. A run on a company results in a significant withdrawal of policyholder funds to the point at which, in one case, a State Insurance Commissioner had to step in to keep a company from going under. When the CEO of Century learned that one particularly influential field manager was advocating that the managers form some type of organized opposition to the affiliation, he made it a point to have weekly lunches with that particular field manager to make sure he had an opportunity to air his concerns and to understand the broader issues. These meetings succeeded in allaying the concerns of that particular field manager but the tension between the Century COO and the career marketing head inhibited the development of the needed comfort level among members of the career system. The career marketing head eventually had to be replaced.

For the operation to be active in the credit union market, it seemed obvious that the staff building Plan America should be located in Madison. At the same time, the expertise to support face-to-face selling in the market was located in Waverly. This created additional stress in both locations. In Madison, Plan America management people were running hard and needed support and quick turnaround on projects. Meanwhile, Century had recently downsized the organization three times and, with limited resources and time, Plan America did not always get the attention it needed. Furthermore, the "process discipline" of the Century people tended to extend the turnaround time. Century had named a point person to shepherd projects through the organization but it was not until the staff began to see the potential of Plan America that adequate resources were allocated to the operation. After about a year of operating the Plan America pilot program, the results were behind the business plan but it became apparent to senior management and the boards what the market potential was and that there were obviously going to be additional synergies by consolidating the resources of the companies. Fortunately, the companies had established ad hoc committees that could keep up in their dialogue with the pace of change. Because of the potential synergies the companies decided to go beyond the concept of the original marketing agreement and to pursue a closer working relationship which would be to the mutual advantage of both parties.

One of the difficulties with pursuing a closer working relationship between the two companies sooner than originally anticipated was the reaction of the Century field force. During the first year of the pilot program there was some misunderstanding on the part of the field force as to the focus by the Century company management. However, Century did not devote more than ten percent of its resources to the pilot program the first year. Nevertheless, the attention it received in publications, the movement of some field underwriters into the program, the focus of the senior management on the project and occasions on which a field underwriter was looking for support and found that the individual needed was "gone to Madison" did not help their understanding. Furthermore, because Century had been very open with the field force, many of them knew that the results were behind plan and that the products sold were different than a career agency system educated on "needs" selling generally sold. Frequent meetings were held with managers by the CEO, COO, and senior vice president (SVP) of marketing to explain the program. Joint meetings were held with groups of agencies by the CEO and the SVP Marketing.

At one particular meeting in Waverly, with the leading field manager and the leading agent in attendance, the CEO was asked what the back-up plan was if the Plan America marketing plan and a closer working relationship with CUNA Mutual did not work. The CEO told them that management had considered all of the alternatives, and had reviewed the dilemma of the industry and had concluded that there was no back-up plan — THIS MUST WORK.

Some staff members at Century felt confident about their capacity to succeed on this project because of what they had already accomplished specifically through the work of their Project Steering Committee (PSC). This, as described in Chapter 5, was an interdepartment discipline that had been established about five years prior to the affiliation. Instead of corporate resources being functionalized, this was an effort to pull together the necessary resources in a timely fashion to complete a project that was essential to the corporation's future. This approach was originally initiated because the market was demanding a quicker turnaround in product development than what had traditionally been the case in the industry. This project management discipline was seen in Century as an effective management tool for the allocation of the company's limited resources. The CUNA Mutual staff, for the most part, had not experienced this same degree of constraint on resources and the difference in the cultures created some tension between the staffs.

Even with the use of this approach it was often difficult to get the necessary support needed for a project that was moving as quickly as Plan America. There were a number of reasons for this. One reason was that Century had downsized several times leaving limited resources to work on the project. Another reason was that Century was disciplined to be more process driven than market driven and thus the demands of Plan America were upsetting to some individuals who wanted to spend more time in analysis. As we point out in Chapter 9, it probably would have been better at this point to "overstaff" and dedicate the additional resources to this project.

One of the frustrations on the part of those who were intimately involved in the project was to witness others who were not involved pointing to the things that were not going well instead of applauding all that had already been accomplished. Part of this was a natural fear of the unknown and the fear of realizing that if this venture was very successful it would ultimately mean change.

To those who were close to the project it was apparent, based on the vision that had been established for Plan America and the strong business plan to support it plus the intimate understanding of the project by both boards of directors, that the project was of strategic importance to both companies and that it would be a "go."

COMPANIES AGREE TO AGREE AND DESIGN/BUILD AFFILIATION

One of the meetings of the joint ad hoc committees of the Boards was held in Chicago in August 1988. It was apparent from that meeting that CUNA Mutual would not proceed with the affiliation unless they could have assurances that Century would not someday try to go it on their own in the credit union market. The Century board knew that such "assurances" might involve some issues of company control, and so they decided to have a special Century board meeting, the purpose of which was to reexamine all of the alternatives available to Century to determine if affiliation were truly in the best interests of the policyholders. To make the analysis as objective as possible, the Century CEO suggested that his COO do the study under the direction of the chairman without any of the CEO's involvement and that a well-known consulting actuary be retained to prepare a report to review the state of the industry and to comment in executive session to the board on the analysis by the COO. At that same meeting, the chief financial officer, on direction from the chairman, was asked to prepare the case for the affiliation. It was apparent that face-to-face selling in the credit union marketplace had tremendous potential for both companies. There were almost 4,000 credit unions in the country that were large enough to support a Plan America representative. In addition there were twice that many that were smaller where a representative could cover several credit unions on a part-time basis. Furthermore, the typical career agent in this country sold, on average, one policy a week. The objective of selling four policies a week in a sponsored market on a "needs" basis definitely seemed attainable. Thus it would be possible to reduce the distribution cost per sale because of the higher productivity.

In addition, it was anticipated that by concentrating the individual insurance processing in Waverly, the group insurance processing in Madison, and the property and casualty processing in Southfield, Michigan, the entire consortium of companies could effectively improve productivity by over $20 million over a period of years. Truly the combination of these pieces could build a sustainable future for both companies.

It was therefore decided to proceed with a permanent relationship. As we have discussed earlier, mergers rarely optimize their objectives and joint ventures are often too tenuous. The reason many mergers fail to reach their objectives is that there is a tendency to turn the process over to the legal and financial staffs and to get "structure" ahead of "strategy." Joint ventures often tend to be centered around the personalities of the CEOs and, when the CEOs move on, the joint ventures tend to come apart. After much deliberation, it was decided to structure this relationship as a permanent affiliation and to keep the focus on strategy instead of structure. The form that the affiliation eventually took grew out of a series of discussions that had taken place between the CUNA Mutual CEO and the CEO of Nationwide Insurance, who had engineered a similar relationship involving his company and another organization. This idea constituted an important breakthrough in the developing relationship between Century and CUNA Mutual because, up until then, the boards of the two companies were favoring two different relationships: the Century Board was in favor of a joint venture and the CUNA Mutual Board was in favor of a merger. The permanent affiliation idea lay somewhere between these two possibilities.

To help the companies refine their relationship and keep their focus on the strategy, each company retained three consultants: an actuary, a certified public accountant, and a lawyer. Their responsibility was to look over the shoulders of the management, the ad hoc committee, and the board as the companies worked through the development of this relationship. The consultants also reviewed the material and meetings in which the companies independently considered other alternatives that would build a sustainable future.

In December 1988 the companies signed a document stating their intention to "agree to agree." This set the course to make sure that the companies accomplished their objective on behalf of the policyholders, to put aside ego-based concerns, potential power struggles and so on. The agreement specified the penalties that would be incurred if either party decided for some reason to abort the plan. In effect the companies decided to "design/build" the affiliation.

What this meant was that the ultimate organization in all its detail was not yet determined but as the companies were putting together the affiliation (that is build) they would determine details (that is design) as they proceeded. The item that was agreed to was the strategy but the structural questions would be determined as they proceeded. This notion had a profound effect on the staff because normally one would ask the question, "What if this doesn't work?" or "What is the back up plan?" But, in this case, there *was* no back-up plan. Once this hurdle was crossed and the staff understood that "we will *make* this work," it had a tremendous impact on productivity. If problems surfaced, and of course they did, the attitude always was how to make it work instead of considering giving it up.

One of the actuaries from CUNA Mutual recalls that at first he struggled with the concept of design/build thinking that more analysis should precede any final commitment to launch the affiliation. However, he eventually reasoned that from a long-term business view one could not simply look at return on investment but must also realize that the baby boomers were soon going to run out of the need for credit and would begin to be more interested in vehicles for accumulation. This would mean that it was important for CUNA Mutual to move into individual face-to-face selling in order to retain a strong position in its market. Furthermore, he concluded that, even though there was an overcapacity (too much staff, technology, and office space) of individual insurance in the country and a lot of mutual companies selling essentially the same product to a limited market, the Plan America operation had something unique, a sponsored market, and, therefore, offered the potential of a reduced distribution cost.

During the months following the "agreement to agree" the ad hoc committees of the two companies met frequently and jointly. Not only did they set the parameters for determining how the strategy should proceed but in effect they began to shape the culture for the joint effort by setting an example for staff of how they were working together to accomplish a worthy objective. For example, it was the joint ad hoc group that defined the general parameters for selecting personnel from the two companies where it was prudent to consolidate some functions.

The process for selecting staff to run the affiliated companies will be explained in greater detail in Chapter 7 under Succession Management, but in general what was decided was to first define the responsibility of the position. Second, all candidates for each position were given psychological assessments as well as assessments to determine their potential for growth in the future. In effect, a "player draft" from each company was then conducted to make sure the best individual was assigned to the position in the affiliation, thus minimizing some of the politics normally found in this type of joint effort.

DUE DILIGENCE

Because the companies were going to establish a permanent relationship it was necessary to conduct an exhaustive due diligence. The purpose of this effort was, to the extent humanly possible, understand all of the financial, administrative and cultural nuances of each company in order that the affiliation might have a high probability of succeeding and that the policyholders of the companies would be protected. To do this each company established an internal team to conduct the due diligence on the other company, and these teams were supported by the outside consultants that the Board ad hoc committees had retained. In effect the work and the results were to be treated like an exhaustive audit with appropriate management letters, and so on. The companies had progressed to the point in their relationship however that the affiliation was going to proceed unless the due diligence effort turned up something significant.

Each of the companies appointed an individual to be the point person for their respective company's due diligence. The two companies appointed individuals who had comparable backgrounds in finance and who were in middle management. When the CUNA Mutual appointee was asked to take the assignment he was to leave on an already delayed vacation to Hawaii the next day. He was asked by his CEO to meet with the Century CEO to get an understanding of the task. The Century CEO, in turn, discussed the project with him and gave him a five page spread-sheet of the assignment as conceived by the individual that was to be his counterpart at Century. He took the material with him on his vacation and was ready to hit the ground running when he returned. It was fortunate that not only were the professional backgrounds of the two individuals similar but so were their personalities. They provided an excellent basis for the process to run smoothly.

From the perspective of one of the company's actuaries, the due diligence was a greater effort than if one were simply doing a merger. In a merger one examines the fairness at a particular point in time but in an affiliation one has to determine the continuing long-term fairness to the policyholders to protect their interests. Furthermore, no specific guidelines exist as to how this should be done through a reinsurance arrangement and what would happen if it would have to be "undone." In the actuary's opinion, the project would not have been completed so efficiently if there had not been a lot of goodwill on the part of both parties.

One of the cultural differences between the companies which showed up in conducting the due diligence itself was the project management system. Also at the time, to the CUNA Mutual staff, the affiliation project was not as critical to long-term survival as it was to Century. Therefore while the due diligence process was thorough in the minds of the CUNA Mutual staff this was a "done deal" and they would have had to discover something significant in order to abort. This is not to say that some important issues did not surface. One example is that, before the due diligence had begun, Century had retained a consulting firm to validate their concern with the marginal profitability of their own products. During the due diligence, CUNA Mutual retained a different consulting firm to independently re-evaluate these findings. Such important issues were studied in depth and this required resources and slowed the affiliation process.

Confidentiality does not permit the disclosure of the findings of the due diligence but at the end of this chapter, we have provided a list of the topics covered. Suffice it to say that, because the companies had always been good stewards of their resources, there was nothing in the reports that would suggest the companies should not proceed with the affiliation. The reports were treated like a "management audit" and were discussed in great detail with the ad hoc committees and in a follow up discussion with each board.

When the due diligence reports were discussed, the subject of cultural differences tended to be more "gray" than "black and white" as would be the case if one were reviewing the financials. While it was important that the discussions regarding cultural differences be held to provide mutual understanding they were not always easy to handle. For example, each CEO would report to his respective board ad hoc committee and would discuss in detail the differences in culture and management style. The two board ad hoc committees would then discuss the differences jointly without the CEOs where it involved differences in management style. These were very open discussions and positive as far as the success of the affiliation was concerned but at times it created some misunderstanding between the CEOs. In effect it was a critique of the particular management style of each CEO.

Considerable concern was expressed at one particular joint meeting of the ad hoc committees in Seattle. Each CEO had met with his own ad hoc committee. In the joint meeting it became apparent that some discussion was needed about the perceived differences in management style between the two CEOs. It was at this point that the board members requested an executive session without the CEOs. In that session they discussed the difference in management styles between the two companies and their leaders. The report of the joint meeting was in turn discussed with each CEO. As a result, the two CEOs met to resolve the issue. The chairmen of the boards of the two companies also participated in the discussions, and, in the final analysis, all agreed that the potential benefit to the companies and their various constituencies was so great that they would continue the process.

The affiliation was a growth experience for many of the staff members involved from both companies. For example, the individual at Century who was responsible for following up on all of the details of the due diligence for Century recalls that this period was a real growth period for him personally. He indicated that the growth went in spurts. There were times when he felt he had a handle on exactly what shape the affiliation would take and then through discussions and analysis there would be new insights and the vision of what the affiliation would be like would change.

During the approximately seven months it required, the due diligence effort produced a great deal of mutual respect among most of those involved and much of this feeling carried over into the affiliation. It was fortunate that it did because difficult times were still to come. After the due diligence was completed, three individuals from each company began working on the affiliation agreement. These sessions resulted in some outright arguments about not only philosophy and concept but sometimes even style of writing. When the discussions reached an impasse the issus would be directed to the CEOs who would always ask, "How can we work through this?" The question of mutual trust would occasionally surface but it was never a question of giving up. Substantive disagreements had to be resolved because, once again, the driving force and the fundamental vision was what was best for the policyholders.

INTENSE STAFF INTERACTION AND NETWORKING

Once the board ad hoc committees had signed the "agreement to agree" and an attitude of design/build was established, there were some corporately sponsored and some department sponsored meetings between staffs. In Chapter 7 we will discuss the interaction of the investment and legal staffs since they were the initial phases of formal affiliation between the companies. There were several sessions held midway between Madison and Waverly of approximately the top twenty members of each company's staff. These were held in Dubuque, Iowa, or Galena, Illinois, and were later referred to as the "Dubena" meetings. Other meetings established by the Human Resources, Information Systems, Financial, and Policy service department head counterparts were held in Dubuque, Madison, or Waverly. The purpose of these meetings was to become better acquainted and to determine if there were ways in which the participants could help each other.

The purpose of the original Dubena meeting was to get acquainted and to give forthright impressions of the other company, both strengths and weaknesses. One very productive activity included having the executives divide into company groups and develop a list of the characteristics of their own and the other company's cultures. These lists were then shared and discussed in detail between the company groups. The senior marketing officer for Century, who had come to know many of the CUNA Mutual people because of his Plan America responsibilities, recalls that the mind sets of the two staffs were different as they approached that meeting. CUNA Mutual had a history of joint ventures to satisfy the needs of their market and, in the words of one senior manager, "we perceived this as a very heavy duty effort and more than just a joint venture." Nevertheless, it was still one in a series of activities to most of the CUNA Mutual people. On the other hand, this was a once-in-a-lifetime experience to most of the Century people. It was obvious that there was much to do to coordinate the thinking of the two staffs in order to develop arrangements that would benefit both parties and therefore communications and dialogue between the staffs would be essential. An important example of the type of issue discussed was one involving the identification of the "customer" in the credit union market. The Century people, coming from an individual life and health orientation, suggested that the credit union member was the appropriate customer, but the CUNA Mutual people, who of course knew the credit union marketplace well, started from the assumption that the credit union itself was the customer. Such issues were very significant and discussion of them allowed the staffs of the two companies to learn a great deal about each other.

The second meeting was to continue the dialogue of where the companies were going with the affiliation and what impact that would have on each company. Counterparts from the two companies met in small groups to discuss specific topics and reported back to the entire group. In these meetings the concept of how far to go in integrating the two companies evolved. That is, legally, there would be two separate entities, but there would be functional integration where possible. Much of this will be become clearer in Chapters 7 and 8. Since there were three distinct lines of business, that is, group billing for credit insurance, individual property and casualty, and individual life and annuities it seemed obvious that the administration and processing of these lines would stay separated. Senior management for the affiliation would have to be integrated, and some functions, such as financial management, audit, information systems, and marketing would present opportunities to enhance productivity through consolidation. Such steps would need to be considered carefully, however, because it was desirable to have some elements of these functions remain in the proximity of the administrative users. A third, corporately sponsored meeting was held in Madison. The purpose of that meeting was to share the lessons learned to date and to discuss how the process might be improved as things proceeded.

One of the outcomes of these meetings was that the staffs of both companies began to describe their strategy as a "soccer ball" approach, with different lines on the ball representing different functions while the ball itself remained one entity. In that context, the legal entities were defined as separate, the financial entities as overlapping but operationally functioning as one and the management structure as the soccer ball. This was a new concept and difficult to understand. It was discussed at length by some participants during the first meeting. They finally agreed that the senior officers who had attended the meetings would discuss the issues of concern with their subordinates, keeping in mind the overall objective but that the discussions would not go into the details. While many communications sessions were held, the novelty of the approach, the complicated nature of the affiliation, and the fact that management did not have all the answers but still shared information on a "need to know" basis created some natural anxiety. While Century's approach involved more "face-to-face" communications sessions than did CUNA Mutual's "written memo" approach, there was naturally greater anxiety at Century than at CUNA Mutual because they would in the final analysis experience the greatest change. In this sense, given the greater impact on the bulk of the Century employees, they had a greater "need to know" than did most of the CUNA Mutual people.

During these sessions the CEOs had decided to refrain from talking and let the staff discuss the issues without prejudicing their opinions. One issue that became the focal point of a cultural difference was the question of who the company's customer was. In CUNA Mutual, it was the credit union and at Century it seemed to be the policyholder. Obviously, in a sponsored market like the credit unions it would have to be the credit unions or the company would forfeit its sponsorship. However, for a company operating in a nonsponsored market, the answer to the question Who is the customer?" may not be so clear. Most insurance companies state publicly that their customer is the policyholder, but as we noted in Chapter 4, some companies functioned as if their agents were the customers. Some of the companies who built career agencies went to the expense of recruiting and training agents and, particularly in recent years, did not control the activities of the agents. The agents had to be treated with "kid gloves" because even though the company had gone to the expense of developing and supporting the agents, some of them wrote business with whatever company gave them the best deal or the best product. Century had had a history of doing somewhat the same thing, but the fact that Century was now pursuing a course of action, the affiliation, that would lower unit distribution costs instead of continuing to build a career distribution system indicates that the company had decided that the policyholder was, in the final analysis, the customer. In the Plan America program the individual policyholder would be writing the check for the coverage. It was obvious that to be successful the companies needed to meld the two philosophies on this issue.

STATE APPROVALS

It was necessary throughout the affiliation process that the legal counsels from both companies stay in continuous contact with the Insurance Departments of the respective states. Ultimately the State Insurance Departments had to approve the transaction. Therefore, it was essential that the Insurance Department not only be apprised of the current transactions but that they have an understanding of the long term vision. The primary interest of Insurance Departments is to protect the policyholders and, therefore, assure prudent management in the state of domicile. At the same time they want to maintain their sphere of impact on the industry in their particular state. During the time of the affiliation there was a general economic downturn in the midwest, and states were urged to find ways to enhance job opportunities. In Iowa one of the primary businesses in the state was insurance and what Century was trying to do was expected to increase employment significantly in the community of Waverly.

The task of clarifying to the insurance departments what the companies were trying to do was not an easy job. The fact that the affiliation was something new created its own set of problems. Both departments were patient in working through the issues, and it probably helped that the two states were in close proximity geographically and had worked together on other issues. While a block of business was to be moved to Waverly, which meant an increase in staff, there would also be a movement of senior staff to Madison which meant that the Iowa Department probably had the hardest task in approving the affiliation.

The Iowa Insurance Commissioner was supportive and focused on the long-term growth in jobs in Iowa and on the long-term enhanced value to the consumer. The Iowa Chief Examiner struggled with the approach probably because he was focusing, rightly so, on the current financials. In effect he was asking why one of the strongest and best managed companies in Iowa would go through all of this change. The legal counsel for Century, together with the oversight lawyer, did a masterful job of working with counsel for the department in walking through each step of the process. No serious objections were raised at a hearing in Des Moines, Iowa and it was made perfectly clear that no one individual profited by the transaction and that the winners would be the policyholders.

The CUNA Mutual staff had a history of working closely with the Wisconsin Insurance Department because of the complex business it was running and the proximity of the Insurance Commissioner's office made it easy to keep in contact. The legal counsel from CUNA Mutual had kept the insurance department posted on each step that was being taken in the affiliation. Therefore, the Wisconsin Insurance Commissioner understood the affiliation process from its beginnings and was very supportive.

The State Departments approved the transaction subject to the approval of the policyholders of the two companies.

APPROVAL BY THE POLICYHOLDERS

An exhaustive description of the details of the affiliation was sent to the policyholders of both companies. At the same time the senior officers held information sessions with the field force to make sure they could answer the questions raised by policyholders. The material that was sent out was also reviewed by the Insurance Departments and the oversight consultants. Information sessions were also held with other interested groups such as retired directors of the two companies. In May 1990, three and one-half years after the initial discussions at Harvard, the policyholders of both companies approved the affiliation by a vote of over nine to one.

COMMUNICATING TO THE CONSTITUENCIES: "C-DAY"

A number of factors tended to facilitate implementing the affiliation, as mentioned previously, which helped the companies make significant progress.   The two companies had evolved in two somewhat similar environments—rural midwest. The plane that Century owned made it easier to respond to difficulties as they arose. They of course were both mutual companies and had a history of dedication to their policyholders. In spite of these common characteristics there were differences that tended to cause problems.

One difference showed up in communications. At Century, communications had become quite disciplined, and all members of the staff were usually informed as needed. Part of this culture at Century evolved during the significant changes that had been made during the five years prior to the affiliation discussions. Nevertheless, as we discussed earlier, in the case of the affiliation, the management of CUNA Mutual sometimes had more information than did their counterparts at Century.

It became obvious that it was necessary for the communication staffs of both companies to begin to work together in a joint effort on almost a daily basis so that information could be communicated effectively throughout the affiliated companies. One lesson Century had learned was to have a consistent, thorough, and detailed communications plan. As a result of the influence of some of Century's Human Resources people, such a plan was implemented in Waverly and Madison after all of the necessary approvals by the state and policyholders had been received and the day on which much of the communication took place was often referred to as "C-day", in which the C stood for communications. The sequence of communications was very important. The first step was to have all of the management staff together to share the information and discuss any issues so that they would be in position to answer any questions from their staffs when the general announcement was made. At the same time, all field managers received a voice mail message, followed up by a memo, so that they would be in a position to answer questions from agents when the announcement was made. The community press and trade journals received the information twenty-four hours after the staff had all received the information so that staff did not first receive the information in the press but rather were "in the know" beforehand.

While there was yet much to do, the companies had already accomplished a great deal in improving productivity and building a sustainable strategy. Because they had established a design/build mode of operation, some of the integration had been accomplished by the time of the policyholder approval. The companies recognized that if they had not been successful in securing policyholder approval they would have had to "unwind" the integration they had initiated. The details of the initial integration will be discussed in Chapter 7 and the ongoing process will be discussed in Chapter 8.

APPENDIX: DUE DILIGENCE TOPICS

The due diligence reports covered the following topics:

1. A review of the chronology of the relationship between CUNA Mutual and Century Companies to in effect audit the strategic positioning of the companies.
2. A detailed review of the insurance environment and the strategic foundation for the permanent affiliation.
3. Nature of the affiliation and resulting implications for the scope of the due diligence process.
   a. Take reasonable steps to determine that the companies could perform their obligations under the affiliation and ensure that they would be able to meet their financial requirements.
   b. Take reasonable steps to determine that there were no significant, previously unknown issues which should be considered in agreeing to the affiliation.
   c. Take reasonable steps to determine that the cultures of the two companies were not incompatible.
   d. Design control processes to adequately protect the policyowners of both companies.
4. The concept of policyowner equity was considered and evolved throughout the process.
   a. Ensure that there would be created a well-conceptualized system to equitably allocate results of shared activities back to each entity.
   b. Ensure that there would be conflict of interest standards that must be observed by all employees of the two companies acting on the behalf of both companies.
   c. Ensure that there was provision for decisions which would apply to dividend policy and which represented a significant feature protecting existing policyowners.
   d. Ensure that there was an allocation of investment opportunity procedure that would provide equitable treatment of each company's policyowners.
5. Ensure that there was an effective cross-reinsurance process that protects the interest of the policyholders.
6. Review the process for issuing credit union business as opposed to business from the career distribution system to make sure there was equity for all concerned.
7. Review termination provisions in the event that the affiliation should fall apart.
8. Review the economy of scale projections and the benefit that would accrue to current policyholders.
9. Review the business transfer provisions to ensure that the process was feasible and would benefit policyholders.
10. Make sure that the companies were addressing all of the human resource issues to ensure that the companies' cultures were compatible.

11. Review the thoroughness and effectiveness of the communications plan for the affiliation to all interested parties.
12. Review again the Plan America results to ensure that the key linchpin to the affiliation was reasonable and attainable.
13. Review again the credit union environment and its potential acceptance of the affiliation.
14. Review the impact of any consolidation of the credit unions in the country on the affiliation in the long term.
15. Review the process for resolving potential conflicts in the affiliation.

7

Forms of Integration in the Affiliation

In Chapter 6 we explained the evolution of the affiliation. In the design/build concept, as defined in that chapter, we described the building phase of the affiliation. Chapter 7 does not chronologically follow Chapter 6. Rather, in this chapter we will go back and describe in detail some of the "design" features that occurred as the affiliation was being "built."

NATURE OF THE AFFILIATION

First of all it may be helpful to the reader if we give a broad overview of the nature of the affiliation. It was decided that the form of the affiliation would cover (a) a joint marketing arrangement within the credit union system in America, called Plan America; (b) integration of the financials through a reinsurance concept; (c) functional integration of management and the board; (d) creation of "communities of interest" in Southfield, Michigan; Madison, Wisconsin; and Waverly, Iowa; and (e) retention of the legal entities of the corporations in their states of domicile.

The concept behind the Plan America operation was discussed in Chapter 6 and will be summarized later in this Chapter. The integration through reinsurance provided additional glue to the permanence of the affiliation. Fifty percent of the individual insurance written by each company was reinsured in the other company and of course fifty percent of the business written in the new market was placed in each company. It was often said that to "undo" a relationship that had been established using this type of reinsurance concept would be like trying to unscramble a scrambled egg. The unusual concept that was used had been identified by the CUNA Mutual CEO. He had his staff review variations of the format used in another major insurance company combination, and it was very effective in accomplishing the affiliation.

Functional integration was implemented under the fundamental concept that "strategy" precedes "structure." The concept was to try to avoid the pitfalls into which mergers and joint ventures often fall. The primary question always asked was where could the greatest economies for the policyholders be generated. The division into "communities of interest" also followed this fundamental concept. Individual property and casualty was the focus and expertise in Southfield, Michigan. Coverages having to do with the credit union as a business, such as the fidelity bond, pensions, group health, and so on, where the market and obvious customer was the credit union, were the focus and expertise in Madison, Wisconsin. Individual life and annuity was the focus and expertise in Waverly, Iowa.

STRUCTURAL RELATIONSHIP

Strategically, it was important that CUNA Mutual retain its identity because it was well known in the credit union market, and it was important that Century retain its identity because it had a recognized quality rating in the individual insurance market and ratings had become significant in an intensely competitive market. Therefore, it was considered necessary that each company retain its legal identity in the affiliation.

In addition, since CUNA Mutual's only market was the credit unions, it was imperative that it retain an element of control over any company that it brought into the market. At the same time it was important to Century to improve the productivity of the distribution system and the only way to do that was to enter a "sponsored" market. Therefore Century would have eleven board members and six would come from the CUNA Mutual board. The remaining five members from the Century board would be added to the CUNA Mutual board. This assured permanence to the relationship in the credit union market.

It was the issue of board membership that created the most anxiety for the Century people. In fact, when the CEO from Century offered to sit down with retired directors of Century to explain what was being done, it was apparent that they were most concerned with the idea that the company was "giving up control." In addition, while the State Insurance Commissioner could see the opportunities for not only Century Companies, but the Waverly community, and Iowa in general (which has always been recognized as an "insurance state"), the chief examiner struggled with the decision. The chief examiner recognized Century as one of the stronger companies in the state and one which needed very little state supervision. The controller for Century, who could see the impact that this move would have on the future of Century, stated that the difficulty the CEO had was that he frequently found it easier to explain the affiliation in terms of what it was not, (that is, it is not a merger, it is not an acquisition, and so on). This was true because most individuals were focused on the company's status today, and if companies were in trouble they would typically merge and then give up control. Here was a company that was apparently not in trouble, certainly not in the near term. The controller often compared the communications dilemma to the case in which one was buying a Cadillac, and, when asked what he was buying, referred to the purchase as not being an Oldsmobile and not a Chevrolet, and so on. He said if the CEO had not established a strong element of trust over a period of years, the affiliation could not have been accomplished.

Over time it was intended that in addition to functional integration in the various sites of "community of interests," the affiliation would evolve to one CEO for the affiliation and senior vice presidents with affiliation-wide functional responsibilities in Madison. This phase of the affiliation will be covered later in this chapter and in Chapter 8.

PLAN AMERICA CONCEPT

The key linchpin for building a sustainable future for both companies and the primary focus of the affiliation was to build a market system for the sale of life insurance, annuities, and securities to individual members of credit unions in this country. In a sponsored market, a higher level of productivity could be achieved than has been the case for life insurance companies in general.

While attempts have been made to improve productivity in a sponsored market in this country, none had achieved the success of one in Australia and one in England where the average number of sales achieved was seven per week. This compares to one a week for the traditional insurance salesperson in this country. To make sure the company understood the reason for the success of the Australian and English stories, staff visited both operations. Because of the affiliation's emphasis on addressing the total financial needs of the membership instead of simply selling products, it was decided to set an objective of four sales per week.

With a goal of 4 sales per week, the compensation level was designed to achieve a desirable mix of business and was part base salary and part commission. The total pay-out was designed to be no more than seventy-five percent of the amount traditionally paid for distribution of life insurance in this country. The extra margin, which is desperately needed in the marketplace today, is intended to provide some compensation to the sponsoring system and to enhance the margin for the two companies but, most important, to provide added value to the customer that could not be acquired in the market in general.

If membership in any given credit union were approximately 3,000, it was felt that was sufficient to justify placing an agent in the credit union. Smaller credit unions were expected to be serviced by traditional career agents from within the Century system.

COMMUNITIES OF INTEREST

The major concern in structuring the affiliation continued to be making sure that "strategy preceded structure." However, it became obvious that significant economies could be achieved by distributing the administrative work that was now being done in three locations to communities of interest where there was a strong core of expertise in a particular line of business. The individual property and casualty administrative work was to be located in Southfield, Michigan, the individual life and annuity administrative work in Waverly, Iowa, and the credit union corporate and group-type administrative work in Madison, Wisconsin. Consistent with the design/build concept, it was decided to proceed with this phase of the integration even before the affiliation agreement had been finalized because initial studies demonstrated the obvious benefits to the policyholders of both companies. In Waverly it meant, for example, almost a 250 percent increase in employment in the near future and, over the long term, something approaching a $20 million improvement in productivity to the benefit of the Century policyholders.

Combining individual administrative functions in Waverly was started as soon as it was apparent that the affiliation would realize substantial savings. By the consolidation of the administrative work from three locations into one there were fewer total staff members needed and the utilization of the particular expertise in this labor-intensive function would save a substantial amount each year. The transfer was done over a period of approximately three years and only after there was adequate training of staff. It was also done in small "chunks" so as not to disturb service to the policyholders. A few administrative professionals from Southfield and Madison transferred with the business to Waverly. Initially the service work was identified as a separate unit in Waverly but further synergy was expected as familiarity evolved and thus additional expected savings would be realized.

When it came time to move the blocks of business and all of the necessary records from Southfield to Waverly concern was raised as to how the records could be moved without disrupting service. The individual in Waverly who was assigned the supervision of the new blocks of business decided that the safest and most expeditious manner was simply to rent a truck, and so the employees themselves moved the records of over 250,000 policyholders during a single weekend. Some staff from Waverly had previously been flown to Southfield to make sure that they could, on the Monday following the move, handle all of the nuances for this block of business so that they would not miss a working day for the consumer. This is but one example among many of the countless hours on nights and weekends that were put in by the staffs in Madison and Waverly to make the affiliation a success.

BOARD MEMBERSHIP

Prior to the affiliation process, the board membership of Century had been gradually allowed to reduce through attrition. The purpose of letting the size of the board gradually decrease was to keep the options open for the Century board since it was not known what the future might hold with respect board size and makeup. By the time the affiliation was to become permanent the Century board numbered seven including the CEO. As explained earlier in the chapter, to avoid any future boards electing to "go it alone" in the credit union market, it was decided that the Century board should number eleven with six seats being held by CUNA Mutual and five by Century. The history of consolidations in this country shows that board membership tends to be a sticky problem, and if the Century board had not had the foresight to prepare for some type of change in the future, not knowing what it might be, it could have become a significant stumbling block in the affiliation. One of the Century board members had been having problems in attendance because of demands from his own business and he elected to retire from the board. A second member was within two years of his normal retirement on the board and he also elected to retire. That reduced the Century members to the desired five.

CUNA Mutual named the four individuals who had been active on the ad hoc committee plus the then current chairperson and the CEO of the CUNA Mutual board to the Century board. The CUNA Mutual board had numbered fifteen for many years, and the permissible number was raised to twenty following the prescribed method of revision. The remaining original five members of the Century board then became members of the CUNA Mutual board making a total of twenty on that board.

While the remaining five members of the Century board had their board membership roots at Century, several of them had a long-term membership in their own companies' credit unions. The members of the newly combined board set a good example of working together toward a common goal. Board members developed a very collegial manner of working through the issues and representing the policyholders. More than once it was stated by members from both companies' boards that they were trying to reflect the interests of the policyholders and not their personal agendas. The Century CEO once asked an outside consultant, after he had worked with the board, if he could identify which company the individual members came from. He could not. In fact, a few years after the affiliation had become permanent the board chairman of the Century board became the secretary of the board for CUNA Mutual which, under usual governance practices of the CUNA Mutual board, would lead to the chairmanship of that board after a period of six years.

DEPUTY CEO

Before any actual functional integration took place it was decided that each of the CEOs would be placed on the board of Directors and the top management committee of the other company. To give visibility and status to that exchange, each CEO was named the deputy CEO of the other company. Since it was anticipated that eventually the senior management committee for the affiliation would be located in Madison, it was expected that the Century CEO would spend a considerable amount of time in Madison but the CUNA Mutual CEO would spend very little time in Waverly. The rationale for locating the senior management in Madison was not only because of the visibility of Madison as the "center of credit unions in the world" but also because it was also easier to recruit professionals to Madison than to Waverly and the necessary travel required by the professionals was more cost effective when travel was initiated in Madison.

Because of the heavy travel schedule demands of the market, the CUNA Mutual CEO rarely visited the Waverly office, whereas the Century CEO, who did not have the same heavy travel demands on his schedule, spent three to four days a week in the Madison office. To commit that much time to Madison, the Century CEO delegated the day-to-day operation in Waverly to a newly named COO from within the Century organization. A detailed job description was set up for the deputy CEO in Madison and in addition he actively participated in the management policies committee, the governing body inside the office.

The job description for the deputy CEO was to cover areas where it was felt that the Century CEO had particular strengths; namely, the human resource area, financial, actuarial and general management. It avoided areas that had more to do with the administrative group type business which would have been new to him. In particular the Century CEO focused on the internal development of the senior staff, meeting with them quarterly to discuss objectives, monitoring progress, and setting personal development goals. It was intended that the companies would, over a period of a few years, move toward one common senior management. The CUNA Mutual CEO, having spent thirty years in the credit union environment, focused more on marketing and other specifics of the credit union business. As part of developing staff, the deputy CEO in Madison was involved in recruiting a new human resources director. These activities, of course, were approved by the CUNA Mutual CEO, but the intent was to move toward a new management policies committee before the retirement of both CEOs.

Century had used an industrial psychologist in its human resource development program for a number of years. It was decided that CUNA Mutual would follow the same program and the CUNA Mutual deputy CEO worked with the Madison staff and the outside resource in initiating the program. This was to be the basis for picking and developing human resources from both companies to build the management structure for the affiliation. More will be said about this later in this chapter in the section on Succession Planning.

There were some difficulties in implementing the joint responsibility between the two CEOs. The plan was to use the strengths of each of the CEOs to best advantage. However, even though the CUNA Mutual CEO's strength was marketing and the market focus of the credit unions and the Century CEO's was more in the area of financial and human resource development, it was at times unsettling to the CUNA Mutual CEO to have someone else working with the CUNA Mutual staff without his intimate knowledge of the discussions. He felt that the Century CEO's lack of familiarity with the credit union environment limited his effectiveness. The two CEOs agreed to meet on a weekly basis "to keep in touch" on all of the issues. However, that did not work out well because of the requirements of the CUNA Mutual CEO's travel schedule, and some of the CUNA Mutual staff felt they were receiving confusing messages from the dual leadership.

At one point the two CEOs decided to have a management audit to determine what might be the best way to integrate and shape the senior management of the affiliation. That report, in essence, suggested that the CUNA Mutual CEO take the role of "Mr. Outside" and the Century CEO the role of "Mr. Inside." However, the two CEOs were not able to reach agreement on that, and the recommendation, therefore, was never implemented. Instead, it was decided to continue the course they were on and work to develop and name the senior managers for the affiliation. More will be said on this later in this chapter under the title of Succession Planning.

FUNCTIONAL INTEGRATION

There was a continuous effort in a number of functional areas of the companies to focus on opportunities for integrating the two organizations. In the following sections we will describe in some detail the steps taken in the investments and legal functions. We do this, not because they were the most important areas of integration, but because they were the first two areas integrated and provided some useful lessons for the rest of the integration to follow.

These two areas were chosen as the first candidates for integration for several reasons. One was that it was possible to integrate them more easily than would be the case with functions which were more integral to the day-to-day operations of the companies. In addition, the emphases by the two companies in the past had been, appropriately, on different functions. That is, CUNA Mutual's more complex market had required greater emphasis on its legal function than had taken place at Century. Conversely, the nature of some of the products to be marketed jointly by the two companies fit well with the heavy emphasis that Century had been placing on its investment department. Both of these emphases had been dictated by the market and had resulted in particular functional strengths that could be brought to the affiliation. This provided a set of circumstances that facilitated an opportunity to get on with the early stages of the functional integration portion of the affiliation.

FUNCTIONAL INTEGRATION OF THE INVESTMENT FUNCTION

It was felt that since the investment function was essentially a "stand-alone" operation, this function could be integrated early on without disrupting the essential corporate strategy and it would, in turn, cut expenses for the two companies. Century had previously considered moving its investment operations to a larger city because modern technology meant that the proximity to the insurance administrative function was not as critical as it had been in the past and recruiting professionals would be easier in a larger city. In addition, because central management for the affiliation would be located in Madison, it, therefore, seemed logical to proceed with the integration of the investment function in Madison.

Furthermore, it was decided that this part of the integration could be started even before the final approvals had been secured for the affiliation. If it had to be unwound, the investment function for Century could be located in Madison. Since blocks of business were being moved to Waverly for administrative processing, this was also a good will gesture to indicate that the movement of staff would go both ways. This decision, however, created unique problems, some of which will be dealt with in more detail in Chapter 8, but we will describe some of the implications here since they deal with the challenges inherent in a design/build approach. For example, the only issue that was certain was that the investment function would be located in Madison and that the Century senior investment officer would be moving to Madison to head up the joint function for the two companies. No decisions had been made regarding the role the rest of the investment professionals from the two companies would play in the combined operation. This created anxiety on the part of all of these individuals regarding what, if any, roles they would have in the new investment department. This was true for both Madison based and Waverly-based staff.

In fact, this uncertainty extended to the senior investment officer of Century. The primary issue to him was that the style of management of the two CEOs was different. At Century he was used to having the investment function delegated to him with oversight through periodic investment strategy meetings, review of significant investments, review of procedures, and through individual performance appraisals. At CUNA Mutual he felt it would be quite different since the CEO had been the head of the investment function at one time and because he felt there might be a tendency in CUNA Mutual (for market relationship reasons) to make investments within the credit union system that would not optimize return and security, but for which he would still be held accountable. There was a point at which he considered "bolting," but the Century CEO felt his involvement was critical. The Century CEO called for the company plane, which was on a marketing mission in North Dakota, to return to Waverly immediately. The two then flew to Madison before the end of the day to have a frank discussion with the CUNA Mutual CEO to resolve any misunderstandings. As a result, the situation was settled and the integration of the investment function went forward.

The Century investment officer held a series of joint meetings with the entire staffs of the two companies, using some outside expertise, to get them to know each other. In addition the Century senior investment officer convinced the Century investment staff to move to Madison with no ultimate security as to whether they in fact would have a job. One professional took a job in Chicago and the rest moved to Madison. Over a period of several years a series of changes were made, based on personal assessments that were done for all senior staff and based on performance appraisals by the senior investment officer. The assessments were necessary to properly match individuals' capabilities with the responsibilities required in the new expanded jobs. The end result was while there were some reassignments, most of the investment professionals from both companies received new opportunities in the expanded organization.   The documented annual savings after the combination were approximately $500,000.   While the savings were significant for the size of the operation, the reader should understand that the integration of the investment function represented the first thrust where the differences in culture became a serious issue. The Century investment officer probably was at the cutting edge of Century's tougher-minded management in terms of open and honest performance appraisals. On the other hand, some of the investment staff at CUNA Mutual were under the impression that the decision to have the Century officer head up investments and the CUNA Mutual officer head up legal had been something of a "horse-trading" decision. Thus when performance appraisals were done on CUNA Mutual staff, the senior officer did not have the benefit of credibility and some felt that many of his decisions involved favoritism. Furthermore, from the point of view of the Century staff that had moved to Madison, decisions seemed to take much longer because of what they perceived as a greater degree of bureaucracy than they were used to in Waverly. More than one of the staff members considered taking other opportunities during the early phase of the integration.

The investment integration also points to another difference in the cultures of the two organizations and in part explains why there was enough confidence on the part of the investment professionals in Waverly to follow the move to Madison without any guarantees. The CUNA Mutual operation, because it was so intensely market focused, with the resulting need for innovative and creative responses to the market, always had a lot of new ideas and projects under consideration in the organization. These activities tended to involve staff in a variety of activities at any given point in time. Century was, by comparison, a singular line of business and more process oriented. As such they had been able to achieve a disciplined personal development and appraisal focus for staff members. Century's senior investment officer had a smaller staff than most of his company's other officers and was probably the epitome of this discipline and follow through when it came to staff development. Furthermore, some of this focus had been intensified by the "investment physical" conducted at Century (see Lesson 23 in Chapter 9), several years before the affiliation. So, the Century senior investment officer was, in effect, working on building a staff to take on increased responsibility in the future.

INTEGRATION OF THE LEGAL DEPARTMENTS

Like the investment function, it was decided to integrate the legal function since it also was essentially a "stand alone" operation. Recognizing the very special circumstances that existed legally in the multitude of relationships within the credit union system, it was decided that the senior legal officer of the CUNA Mutual would be the senior legal officer for the affiliation. It should also be noted that because of the highly complex organization, the unique coverages provided, as well as varied litigation and regulatory issues with which CUNA Mutual dealt, its senior legal officer had needed to build a competent and professional staff. He had done a fine job of it. Furthermore, as in the case of the investment integration, that is, it would be easier to recruit legal professionals in Madison than in Waverly, the function was to be located in Madison. In addition, it made sense to locate this function in Madison because that was recognized as the "world center for credit unions" and again it demonstrated good faith, since the blocks of business were being moved to Waverly.

The legal integration was done shortly after the investment integration and some of the lessons learned in that first experience were applied in this case. A prototype legal organization was defined first, and then based on individual assessments, staff from the two organizations were selected to fill those positions. Over a period of about a year all of the legal professionals from Waverly were offered opportunities in Madison and all accepted with the exception of Century's senior legal officer. He stayed in Waverly for a short period to help in the transition and then elected early retirement. One of the legal officers from Madison moved to Waverly to be in close contact with the administrative functions there that would be expected to seek legal advice on specific issues.

SUCCESSION PLANNING

Before they retired, the two CEOs wanted to select a senior management core for the affiliation and in that process to develop a succession planning technique that would apply throughout the affiliated companies. If a succession planning process could be established that considered candidates from all three locations for positions in any particular site then real glue would be added to the entire affiliation for the long term.

The framework for the succession planning process was essentially the same as had been established by the board ad hoc committees referred to earlier in this chapter but broadened to cover at least the first three levels of management. An example of how the process was to be utilized throughout the affiliation was established in selecting the senior members of the Management Policies Committee for the affiliated companies. Following is an outline of that process.

1. Individual psychological assessments and behavioral patterns were developed for each of the candidates for the various positions.
2. A team consisting of an organizational change specialist, an insurance organization specialist, the senior Human Resources officer for the affiliated group, the individual who did the assessments, and the two CEOs who, of course, could provide contextual performance input was formed to work through the discipline.
3. The team assigned criteria to each position in the Management Policies Committee that first identified the basic skills needed for any candidate to be considered for a particular position and second defined what skills were needed in each position in the future for the candidate to do an outstanding job.
4. The next step was to try to match the capacity of the individual with the responsibilities needed in the future. The team further tried to define what skills of the individual were basically innate or "hard-wired" where you could expect minimal results from concentrated developmental efforts and which skills were in effect "soft-wired."
5. Candidates were then named to each position, and the results of the analysis were shared with each individual.

Obviously in a disciplined approach like this, one must avoid the pitfall of assuming that the process will come up with all the answers. Some judgment must remain. The process did minimize subjective considerations and probably most important, in the discussion of the results with the candidates specific development plans were laid out for each individual which led to an excellent utilization of human resources.

Out of this process the companies named the senior Management Policies Committee, which covered all of the integrated functions for the affiliated companies, namely marketing, administration, investments, legal, information systems, corporate development, and financial. This process was used in the future as the companies considered various phases of integration.

OTHER INTEGRATION ACTIVITIES

As indicated earlier, other informal efforts at integration were primarily initiated by the senior heads of the functions in the two companies, most notably information systems and human resources.

The respective information systems staff held a series of sessions simply to get acquainted with the state of sophistication of technology in the two companies. At about this same time, CUNA Mutual had retained an outside consultant to help integrate the information systems operation in Southfield with the Madison operation. Because the other "get acquainted" sessions were being held between Madison and Waverly at the same time, a feeling developed that there was an attempt to move the information systems from Waverly to Madison at the same time. Those discussions were premature and were discontinued until a new information systems senior officer had been named for the affiliation. This particular position was filled by an individual from outside of the two organizations. Subsequent analysis suggested the most appropriate integration steps and they are discussed in Chapter 8.

The human resource function took a more deliberate approach to integration. This effort was sponsored by the CEOs. The attempt was started here for several reasons. First, the assessment process and job evaluation systems were a normal function of human resources and it was felt that whatever was learned in this integration could be used as a model as other functions were looked at. Furthermore, a member of the human resources department would be involved as one moved down into the organization with the succession management process. This process, discussed further in Chapter 9, involved analyzing specific responsibilities within the human resources function and negotiating which location would have (a) primary responsibility, (b) shared responsibility, (c) or simply a role of keeping counterparts advised on each function within the human resource role. The result of this effort set a good exaample for other phases of integration.

Efforts were made to encourage some senior staff members from Madison to join the Waverly senior management. Short of forcing such a move this effort failed because it probably appeared to be out of touch with what was happening in Madison, particularly since the two CEOs both spent most of their time in Madison and not Waverly. In addition to the legal officer mentioned under legal integration two middle-management individuals did voluntarily move their families to Waverly and became a part of the operation. One was an actuary and worked with the COO in Waverly. He subsequently, after a two years period, returned to Madison as the assistant to a Management Policies Committee executive. The other individual that moved his family to Waverly was a part of the marketing staff, reporting to the senior marketing officer in Waverly. He subsequently became a field manager in Texas and, still later, moved back to Madison in another capacity.

Another item worthy of note in the integration was the role the senior officers in Waverly played in implementing the vision of the affiliation. The Century CEO was now spending up to four days a week in Madison and had delegated the Waverly operation to an individual on the staff and named him COO. Since the senior investment officer and the senior marketing officer had moved to Madison it meant that new staff members had to assume responsibility in Waverly. It is interesting to note that most of those who took on new responsibilities were a part of the MBA group that had voluntarily worked on the company vision as discussed in Chapter 5.

This new group of officers took on the assignment of trying to define Century's role in the affiliated companies. It was this group that had approved adding the line "An Affiliate of the CUNA Mutual Insurance Group," to the sign at the entrance of the Waverly offices. This had raised additional questions on the part of not only the home office staff but the field people as well. (See Chapter 8.)

The Century controller had once stated, when reflecting upon why so much progress had been made in a relatively short period of time, that the word to both staffs was, "We are supposed to affiliate and not spend our time going back each day to read an agreement as to what are we to do next." The nature of the design/build approach was to focus on achieving the affiliation and not on what to do if it did not work.

In this chapter, we have described the strategic focus of the affiliation and the initial efforts at functional integration. After these initial efforts, and in part as a result of them, a more formal approach to integration began to take shape. This approach was built around the idea that there were three broad forms of integration that could be considered in the case of any particular function: (1) the function should be *consolidated* and have a central location, (2) the function should be *coordinated* from one location, but might be divided among more than one geographical location, or (3) the function should be characterized by *cooperation* but there might be very little, if any, functionally defined reporting relationship established. For example, the legal and investment functions were consolidated in Madison, the labor intensive processing of the blocks of business was consolidated in Waverly, while the human resources function was coordinated from Madison. Other examples will be described in Chapter 8 as we tell the story of continuing integration.

8

Continuing Integration

INTRODUCTION

In this chapter, we will tell the story of the seemingly endless process of integration that Cuna Mutual Insurance Group and Century Companies have undergone. It is, of course, continuing even as we write and it has been difficult for us to decide when to stop the process of updating. At some point it is probably fair to say that the process of integration becomes one of general change. That is, even though things continue to evolve, some distinctions between the two companies have faded to the point at which it becomes difficult to distinguish between changes that are "integration" and those that are simply "evolution" of the type that might occur in any organization. We have tried, nevertheless, to make that distinction here in that we have attempted to limit our discussion to issues that are clearly extensions, or at least outgrowths, of the affiliation of the two companies.

We will begin the chapter with a discussion of some general integration issues that seem to transcend functional or departmental boundaries. Following that, we will focus on the continuing integration taking place in a number of specific functions.

GENERAL INTEGRATION ISSUES

Reengineering

One of the more recent issues to emerge has been the affiliated group's interest in the concept of reengineering. We begin our discussion with this issue even though it is very much out of sequence chronologically, because we believe it illustrates quite well many of the integration-related challenges faced by the two companies.

In the late summer of 1993, Century Companies, now called the Individual Life and Health Division (ILH), decided to become involved in what has come to be called "reengineering." This is a form of organizational change which focuses on the idea of reinventing an organization's ways of doing its work. It involves identifying various "processes" in the organization and then designing the most effective ways of accomplishing the work involved in those processes. A "process" is any group of activities, which may cut across several functional areas of an organization, that takes one or more kinds of input and creates an output that is of value to the customer.

ILH management had decided to become involved in reengineering because it had become apparent that, in order to reach certain cost-reduction goals, some significant improvements in the company's operating efficiency were needed. Much of the literature on reengineering (see, for example, Hammer & Champy, 1993) indicated that, when it was successful, *very* significant reductions in operating costs and equally significant improvements in customer service were possible. Consequently, ILH management had decided that reengineering might offer one way to achieve some of the improvements they wanted. A number of aspects of the affiliated group's experience with reengineering illustrate the challenges of achieving full integration of the two companies.

To begin with, the cost-reduction goals for ILH, which is the Waverly operation, had been established by the Management Policies Committee of the affiliated group. Century's former COO was, in his new role as head of ILH, a member of that committee, and he, as well as others from ILH had been involved in the decision. However, some of the people in Waverly thought it was quite a different experience to be required to achieve goals that had not been set "in Waverly." From the point of view of some of those in Madison, it was also seen as a somewhat different experience. They *had* been in the position before of trying to get management groups in other locations to achieve certain goals, (for example with Pomona, California, and Southfield Michigan), but this situation involved an affiliation. This is a special case of a general issue that has developed as the organizations have continued their integration. That is, what is the relationship between Waverly and Madison? Which decisions are to be made in Madison and which in Waverly? How much autonomy is Waverly to have? This issue crosses all functional areas and, as of this writing, had been clarified to differing degrees depending on the functional areas involved. As Waverly moved ahead with its plans to become involved in reengineering, this issue, as well as others, played a role in their progress.

During the fall of 1993, Waverly moved ahead with reengineering by taking a number of steps. For example, the Waverly Executive Management Committee (EMC) appointed Century's human resources vice president as their reengineering leader. They selected the "order fulfillment" process as their beginning point and they described this process in written communication to all ILH employees in Waverly as follows: "This process begins when an individual decides to make a purchase. It includes both applicants from our face-to-face distribution systems and direct response members. The process ends when two events have taken place: 1. We have received the first premium payment. 2. The applicant has received the policy."

In addition, the EMC selected a reeingineering team that would be reponsible for "reinventing" the order fulfillment process. They physically moved the team members to a location in the downtown building in Waverly.

However, as they were moving ahead, reengineering-related events were also taking place in Madison. It had become clear to the Management Policies Committee in Madison that the entire affiliated group needed to reexamine its ways of operating, and they, like the Waverly group, had decided that reengineering offered a desirable way to do so. The chief marketing officer had already undertaken significant steps to reorganize and integrate the distribution systems which we will be discussing in some detail later in this chapter. In addition, and more directly related to Waverly's reengineering efforts, the head of ILH had also begun to take steps to get underway with a reengineering effort in the operations areas of Individual Life and Health, of which Waverly was a part. The vice president of ILH and his reengineering leader had kept their boss abreast of their plans and progress on reengineering, and he had told them to, "Go ahead and if what you're doing raises questions with what we (in Madison) eventually do, we'll sort it out when the time comes."

Well, the time came very early. For example, the ILH head decided to appoint the former CEO of the League Companies, who had done such excellent work for the affiliated group in taking over management of the Southfield operation, to the position of director of reengineering for the affiliated group. This then raised the question of whether the head of reengineering for ILH would report to the ILH vice president or to the head of reengineering for the affiliated group. This ambiguity, quite naturally, caused the new corporate reengineering head to tell ILH's reengineering head to "put everything on hold until I get my feet on the ground." In addition, the ILH head was telling his reengineering leader that the corporate reengineering head's position was to be a staff position, but the corporate reengineering head was telling him that he felt his positon was a "line management" position. The ILH head was, at the same time, telling his reengineering head that he expected early results and that he was concerned that things were not moving quickly enough. It should be pointed out that we are not suggesting that anyone was at fault here. Quite the contrary. Such difficulties attend almost all combinations of organizations, and in this case, goodwill prevailed, all of this was eventually sorted out, and Waverly moved ahead with their reengineering effort and learned a great deal in the process. In fact, in the late spring of 1994, ILH's reengineering leader accepted a position in Madison as a member of the "core reengineering team" for the entire affiliated group. He retained primary liaison responsibilities with the Waverly reengineering effort and was able, at the same time, to contribute substantially to the overall reengineering effort using what he had learned through his experiences in Waverly.

In addition, there was the matter of consultants. The Waverly management group had decided to move ahead with minimal outside help other than some support from Digital Consulting on the use of reengineering "tools and technology" that Digital had developed. They also had some intermittent help from a consultant they had used for many years on a variety of organizational changes. When the Madison group began to move ahead, they too addressed the issue of the need for outside help, and, for a time, it remained unclear what they were going to do. During that time, the Waverly group became concerned about whether they might be asked to accept the involvement of a consultant not of their choice. This issue became even further complicated when, during this same period of time, the CEO identified and hired another consultant to help him reexamine the top management structure of the affiliated group. Once again, however, good faith and communication resolved this issue.

We use this example to illustrate how much more complex organizational life had become for the people both in Waverly and in Madison as a result of the affiliation. It may be of interest to note that a significant amount of this complexity centered around the role of the former Century COO, who had, of course, come to Madison from Waverly. That is to say, the uncertainty between Madison and Waverly was not because one company was influencing the decisions in another company about which they understood too little. It is our opinion that the uncertainty was a result of structural variables inherent in situations in which organizations come together, even when the parties have worked together for years and know each other well. When the Century COO moved to Madison to become the head of Individual Life and Health he *needed* to take a different and broader point of view, than he had taken as chief operating officer in Waverly and he did so. In addition, he began to appreciate that he was faced with a substantially larger and more complicated organization in Madison. As a result, he found himself at one of the two "vortexes" of integration between the two organizations, that is to say the "operations vortex." The chief marketing officer was at the other one, the "distribution systems vortex," and we will discuss his integration challenges later in this chapter.

The Plane

We mentioned in an earlier chapter that some, including CMIG's CEO, felt that the affiliation may never have taken place if Century had not had a company airplane to facilitate the many meetings that took place at various locations. The plane, of course, has continued to be heavily used as the integration of the companies has progressed. However, in 1993, in an attempt to find ways in which they could reduce expenses, Century management began exploring the possibility of selling the plane. Among the possibilities considered was one of having the CUNA Mutual Group buy the plane from Century.

The concerns that this possibility raised in the minds of some Century associates tell us something about the extent to which the companies may have achieved an optimum level of trust and shared values. To wit, many of the Waverly people were pleased at the prospect that the affiliated group might buy the plane but some also raised two questions: First, what portion of the expense necessary to purchase and maintain the plane would be charged back to Century? Second, we (Century) have been careful to use the plane as a tool. That is, seats on it have been available to anyone, regardless of level in the company, who had a legitimate business need. Would that continue to be the policy, or would use of the plane become a "perk" of top management? Once again, a solution was reached and a plan to deal with these issues was worked out and implemented in the fall of 1994. The plane was not sold, and the plan for its use includes maintaining the day-to-day seat reservations on the plane in Waverly in the hands of the person who had that responsibility before the affiliation, but having the travel function report to the executive offices in Madison for coordination purposes.

The Nature of the Affiliation

As the integration has progressed, many Waverly associates have continued to be concerned about the extent to which Century Companies may be in the process of becoming "just another line of business of CUNA Mutual" or, in a later version, "just a business processing center for Madison." This has been an issue for some Century people at least as far back as the management meetings that were held in Galena and Dubuque. As we have described in earlier chapters, at the first of those meetings the "soccer ball" concept of the affiliation was discussed and, for the first time, it became clear to some of the Century managers that their company was not simply entering into a joint venture with CUNA Mutual, but rather was becoming a part of a group of companies. To one degree or another, the issue of exactly what this means has remained an important one for many Century people right up until the present.

Naturally, as the integration of the two companies has moved forward, many questions concerning the emerging nature of the affiliation have been answered. However, and in spite of the rationale described at the end of Chapter 7, among the concerns that remain, an important one is that in the eyes of some Century people, there seems to be a migration of management people, and thus management control, from Waverly to Madison. It began with the consolidation of the Investment functions of the two companies. As we have described, Century's vice president of investments was selected to head the combined departments which were located in Madison. That was accompanied by the combining of the Legal departments under CUNA Mutual's chief legal officer in Madison. Century's vice president in charge of marketing was given overall responsibility for the joint venture (Plan America) and was relocated to Madison. Later, Century people were pleased to learn that their COO had been offered the position of head of the entire Individual Life and Health business for the affiliated group. They felt that his appointment signaled the importance in the affiliated group of their part of the business. But their enthusiasm was tempered somewhat when it became clear that to accept the position he would have to move to Madison. To make matters worse in their eyes, they learned that although he was to be named president of Century upon their CEO's retirement, there would be no CEO of Century separate from CUNA Mutual. Rather, the CEO of CUNA Mutual would become CEO of Century as well. (It should be noted that this arrangement had been contemplated in the affiliation agreement, which was simply not known by some of the Century people.) Later the investment accounting function moved to Madison. In 1993, the two companies' internal auditing functions were combined under the direction of a Century manager, who also moved to Madison. When still another Century manager was asked to oversee the integration of the two companies' data and voice communications systems, he moved to Madison. Century's mainframe computer was moved to Madison in the summer of 1993. In the summer of 1994, the Century Pension operation moved from Waverly to Madison. In addition, as the chief marketing officer continues to develop the integrated distribution system, the question has arisen as to how much sense it makes to keep the former Century career system marketing support people in Waverly. As of this writing, (April 1995), it is clear that at least some of those people will also be asked to move to Madison.

It should be apparent that when all of these developments are viewed together, it does appear that Waverly is becoming something other than a complete company. What it will eventually become is still not entirely clear. A significant development in this regard took place in July 1993. At that time, Century management announced to all Waverly associates and to the Century field sales people that henceforth, "the credit unions are our customers," and described some of the ways in which taking that position was expected to affect Century structure and ways of operating. This was a very important milestone for Century. As far back as the second management integration meeting in Dubuque, the CMIG CEO had been adamant that the issue of the identity of the customer of the affiliated group was simply not open to discussion. The customer was the credit union. Many Century people were offended by what they felt was the closed-mindedness of that position at that time, but subsequently came to realize that this was a realistic conclusion based on the realities of the credit union market structure. So, for Century management to accept that idea and to move decisively in the direction of implementing changes designed to serve that market as its primary future emphasis was, in some senses, the culmination of years of interaction between the two organizations.

What might this mean for the future of the career agency system in the affiliated companies? Clearly the companies were scaling back the recruitment of career agents. However, they have not abandoned the system in that successful Plan America agents could still transfer to career system status and career agents would continue to receive support, so long as that support was consistent with that needed by the Plan America distribution system.

The ultimate extension of the philosophy of serving the credit unions was announced at the annual CUNA Mutual Management Seminar in December 1993. At that meeting a number of changes that were, or would soon be, underway were discussed. One of them concerned the CEO's desire to reorganize the company around the three major activities carried out by the credit unions: lending, member services, and internal operations. Exactly what this might mean for people in Waverly, as well as many of those in Madison, Southfield, and Pomona, remains to be seen.

PROGRESS ON SPECIFIC ASPECTS OF THE INTEGRATION

We turn now to some more specfic aspects of the continuing integration between the two companies. In particular, we will focus on some developments in internal auditing, information systems, the integrated distribution systems, and some aspects of integration at the top management and board levels.

Internal Auditing

As we mentioned briefly earlier in this chapter, the internal auditing functions of the two companies were consolidated, under the direction of a Century manager in the summer of 1993. The manager and his family moved from Waverly to Madison in August of 1993. He was appointed a vice president, reporting to the chief financial officer for the affiliated group.

This particular integration step is of special significance because of the role played by the internal audit function. When the original negotiations between Century and CMIG began, Century's chief financial officer as well as his staff felt that it was extremely important that the internal auditing functions of the two companies remain independent to ensure that the interests of the policyholders of the respective companies be protected. However, by 1993 they had become convinced that there was no longer reason to be concerned about this issue. Century's current COO, who had been a key player in the affiliation and one of those most concerned with this issue at that time, told us in March 1994 that once the companies had combined the CEO positions (see below) and had developed so many interconnected reporting relationships, the notion of independence of the auditing functions had become an academic one. He felt that the affiliated companies' management still had the responsibility to protect the interests of the policyholders of the respective companies, and that it was incumbent on them to do so in spite of the fact that many of their roles and functions had been combined. He had become convinced that this was not only possible to do, but that it was in fact being done. Furthermore, the board of directors have a covenant with the policyholders of each company and the Agreement of Permanent Affiliation requires "a fair and equitable allocation of all costs and expenses" and the establishment of an oversight function by the respective board audit committees as well as "a review of the systems and procedures by an outside consultant who shall then prepare a comment letter to the audit committee of each company."

Information Systems

We mentioned earlier that the mainframe computer that had been in use in Waverly was moved to Madison in the fall of 1993. We also mentioned that Century's head of information systems (IS) began reporting to the IS head in Madison. These are, of course, just specific features of the general move toward consolidation of the information systems functions of the two organizations.

The reader may remember that in Chapter 7 it was mentioned that Century's head of IS and CMIG's head of IS had been among the very first management people to forge ahead with meetings between their respectives staffs to explore ways in which they might capitalize on the potential synergies offered by the affiliation. At the time, some of the other management people of the companies thought that perhaps the IS people were moving too quickly. However, there was also interest among some CMIG people in trying to take advantage of what was perceived by some to be a "state-of-the-art" client management system that Century was exploring. This particular endeavor turned out to be an expensive and not very productive one for Century, since the vendor organization never delivered the product. In any event, for our purposes in this chapter, it is useful to note that the IS integration efforts have a rather long history in the affiliation.

In spite of that, it would appear that the affiliation was somewhat slow to take full advantage of the potential synergies in this area. As we discussed in Chapter 2, this is one of the failings that is quite common when companies combine and it seems to have taken place in this case as well. However, more recently, substantial progress has now been made. In January 1993, an information systems integration study was begun. It involved establishing five functional study groups within the IS divisions of the two companies so that members of each of the five functional areas from both companies could carry out the study together. This study resulted in the following changes:

1. As mentioned above, the data centers of the two companies were combined and this entailed moving the Century mainframe computer to Madison in September 1993. No people moved from Waverly to Madison but the change did require some movement of people within the Waverly operation.

2. The management and administration of voice and data transmission among the company's locations was combined and a Century manager was appointed to accomplish the integration of these systems. The mechanics of integrating the electronic mail systems were not difficult and this was accomplished fairly promptly. However, achieving optimum use of this system, as well as integrating the voice-mail systems turned out to be rather challenging tasks for two reasons. First, the two companies had different voice-mail vendors, and it required some considerable discussion to reach agreement among all concerned on a course of action. After considering having one or the other company switch over to the other company's system, it was finally decided to leave each company's system intact and to link them with a system called Voice-Mail Link. This was accomplished in March 1994. The companies are still working on the second challenge which illustrates what had been a difference in the two companies' cultures. Most of the Century people have long been regular users of their electronic and voice-mail systems. They send messages on them quite regularly and they check for messages daily. The reasons for this go back at least a decade. At their CEO's urging, most managers at Century had begun using voice-mail in 1983. Likewise, at his insistence, they had begun using electronic mail not long afterwards, and the proactive use of both systems had become very common at Century. By contrast, historically, some CUNA Mutual managers have made less use of such systems. Obviously, any system of communication is effective only if most, if not all, of the organization's members make use of it and significant progress has been made on this count.

3. The senior management of IS was integrated and Century's senior IS officer began reporting formally to the CUNA Mutual IS head in May 1993. In addition to his reponsibilities in Waverly, Century's IS head assumed responsiblity for the IS financial management group in Madison. This group consists of ten people and performs the budgeting and cost allocation work for the affiliated group's IS function.

4. It is expected that the study will be revisited in the future to explore further integration possibilities.

Distribution Systems

It seems clear that no other aspect of the affiliation has created as much concern as the issue of the integration of the distribution systems. Early on, some of Century's field people became concerned when they felt that the company's executives were not sharing as much as they could about the likely form of the relationship between the companies. Their concern seemed to center around their fears that the affiliation would result in the company focusing its resources on distribution approaches other than the Century career system. This, of course, was because of the tremendous emphasis and glowing predictions that were being expressed for the Plan America joint venture.

Put more broadly, their concern was to preserve the identity of their company. Some of them had represented Lutheran Mutual for many years, and they had already gone through a major identity crisis when the company changed its name to Century Companies. But at least they still felt identified with an individual life insurance company with a 100-year history, a strong reputation as a low-cost insurer, and an A+ rating. They felt that their ability to market successfully depended in large part on maintaining that strong, clear, trustworthy image in the minds of the public. Now they were afraid that their company might "disappear" into a larger one, and one that had this special type of market, credit unions, about which most of them knew little or nothing. So, when their home office executives told them that this would be a great opportunity for them, that it would open up a huge new market, they were skeptical. When they were told there would be no reduction in support for them, they were also skeptical.

Most people familiar with the life insurance industry would probably agree that many field people are skeptical about almost everything they hear from their home office. They feel that most of what they hear is hot air and will never take place. As a result, they ignore a great deal of it and go about trying to make a living. But sometimes, when it becomes apparent that there really is something important happening, they become very interested, as well as very suspicious, because they feel that on the really substantive issues, what they are likely to get is not hot air but a snow-job. In the case of the affiliation, it was apparent that something very substantial was afoot and so the Century field people were suspicious. As the outline of the Plan America joint venture took shape, they became even more concerned because it became clear that it was going to require a great quantity of resources, and they were worried that this would mean less support for the career system. However, the home office assured them that the joint venture was going to be very carefully evaluated over a two-year trial period.

After about a year, the company announced that Plan America showed signs of a tremendous future and that it was going to be greatly expanded. This raised the suspicions of some of the Century field people, as well as some others, because it was known that the early production results of the joint venture were not what had first been projected. The real reason that the decision had been made to forge ahead was that top management of both companies had become convinced of the inherent "rightness" of the Plan America concept in spite of the fact that they had not yet been able to achieve the results they wanted. In the CUNA Mutual culture this intuitive feel for the "rightness" of something might have been enough but, in the more data-bound Century culture, it was not. As a result, Century management did not feel they could say they just "knew" it was the right thing to do, so they said their decision was based on results and this engendered distrust among many in the field who had suspected all along that some major decision to go to a new distribution system had been made and that they simply were not being told the whole truth. The management of both companies felt that this decision would ultimately benefit everyone including members of Century's career system. Their reluctance to be more direct was based on their concern that the career system people would not realize early on that such benefits would eventually develop.

As time passed, it became clear that there was a great deal more to the relationship between the two companies than a joint venture. Slowly, the full scope of the affiliation became apparent and, as it did, the field people's identity fears were exacerbated. An event of particular significance to many in both the Century career system and the Waverly home office occurred when the large sign that sits at the entrance to Century's home office was modified to reflect the company's new status as "an affiliate of the CUNA Mutual Insurance Group." As it happened, the sign was modified during a field management school that was being held at the Red Fox Inn, across the road from the home office. When the participants came across the road to the home office for lunch, the sign looked as they had always seen it. However, when they went back a little later, it was being changed and some of them became upset. Why? Because the sign said, "an affiliate of. . .," rather than, "affiliated with . . ." To them, this wording implied some sort of subordinate position and seemed to confirm that their company was being "swallowed up" by CMIG. As usually happens among field insurance people in cases of perceived bad news, some of them got on the phone immediately and, within a few hours, almost the entire field system felt that their fears had come true. To make matters even worse, they soon learned that their business cards would also have to say "An affiliate of the CUNA Mutual Insurance Group." To the field people, these symbols of identity were of particular importance. They imagined themselves trying to market their products and being forced to explain that people could still trust them and their company, even though they were now a part of some other entity about which they, and certainly their clients, knew almost nothing.

The Plan America joint venture was, as we mentioned previously, placed under the direction of Century's vice president of marketing, who moved to Madison. However, it was to be supported in large part by the same marketing people who had been supporting the Century career system and they were to remain in Waverly. A manager on the Waverly staff was to be the liaison and, as such, he was in many senses the only Plan America advocate in Waverly. As we have recounted in Chapter 6, this manager in particular, and Plan America in general, had great difficulty early on in getting the support they felt they needed. For some time, a rather poor working relationship existed between Plan America and the Century marketing department. In spite of this and many other challenges, Plan America continued to grow, and it became apparent to some of the Century field managers and representatives that, if one stayed with the company, the future lay in Plan America. However, it was not yet clear to them exactly how to gain access to it, and, for some, it was not even clear how it could meet their desires to remain as "entrepreneurial" as they wanted to be.

The Century career system regional positions were eliminated. One of the two regional VPs took over the Southeast Iowa agency. The other was asked to play a role in developing the integrated distribution system to be described below. The former Plan America regional officers became the regional officers for a combined Century career/Plan America field system and began reporting to a newly named VP of face-to-face marketing, who, in turn, reported to the head of all Individual Life and Health marketing including face-to-face and Direct Mail. These and other changes caused over a half dozen of Century's more entrepreneurial agency managers to decide during the subsequent couple of years that it would be in their best interests to move to other companies. This was also the case with some of the agents, who felt that as the company focused more and more on the credit union market, their special needs were not going to be well met.

The point of reviewing this history is to demonstrate that the joint venture and thus the affiliation had not been well received by many of the field people and that this has provided a challenge for CMIG management who have been trying to develop an integrated distribution system for the affiliated group. Nevertheless, they have made significant strides which we will review.

As mentioned above, during 1993, the integration of the Plan America and Century Career Systems was begun. Regional VPs were named to whom both Century managers and Plan America managers were to report. In the spring, managers of the two systems met in Denver for the first joint managers' meeting.

In an even more comprehensive integration attempt, the company decided to try to pilot a completely integrated distribution system in one region of the country. This brought together in one structure the Century Career System, the CUNA Mutual Group Field System, and the Plan America Distribution System. The North-Central region was selected and a former CUNA Mutual national account VP and group sales manager was named senior marketing officer for that region in May 1993. Originally, this region was to be used as an extended test site, but by the fall of 1993, it had become clear that credit unions were very pleased with the company's regional marketing concept. Consequently, at the very first Joint Field Management Conference in Madison in October 1993, the chief marketing officer (CMO) announced an "accelerated roll-out" to the entire country of the regional marketing divisions. There were to be eight such divisions, and the CMO announced that he wanted them all operational by June 1994. This was designed to accomplish the complete structrual integration of all three of the face-to-face distribution systems of the affiliated companies. In the January 1994 issue of the *C-Notes*, the Century field news publication, the rest of the eight division senior marketing officers were announced. During February and March regional kick-off meetings were held to introduce the senior marketing officers to their people and to describe the "new way of doing business" that was being launched. This was, of course, a major undertaking and a number of challenges had to be faced, not the least of which was that not all of the people in attendance at these kick-off meetings yet knew whether there would be places for them in the new organization.

The January 1994 issue of *C-Notes* was to be the last. It was replaced by the *Representative's Report* which was the title that Plan America had been using. This publication became the vehicle for sharing news and developments in the affiliated companies with members of the integrated distribution systems.

In August 1994 the two additional sales forces, Individual Property and Casualty and Direct Response Marketing, were also included and the name of the publication was changed to *Connections* to reflect what the new marketing structure was intended to mean for all of the participants, that is stronger connections to each other and to credit unions and their members.

Investments

In Chapter 7, we discussed the early phases of the integration of the investment functions of the two companies. The reader may recall that this was the very first of the functions to be integrated, and that it was, therefore, a particularly challenging undertaking. In this chapter, we want describe how the integration of this function has proceeded and detail some of the continuing challenges faced by the VP of investments and his management team.

As we described earlier, when Century's investment VP agreed to go to Madison and undertake the task of integrating the Investment function, he was also asked by the Century CEO to assume another, and in some ways more challenging, role. This was the role of "cultural change agent." That is, the CEO (and, indeed, many of the Century people) felt that they had developed a culture in their company that consisted of such values as open and direct communication, and a climate for performance in which performance reviews were conducted in a clear, direct manner. This aspect of their culture was something they wanted to preserve because they felt it was something of value that could enhance the growth of the affiliation. It was Century's perception, (not necessarily shared by many at CUNA Mutual), that the CUNA Mutual culture needed to be more like theirs in this regard. The CEO thought that one good vehicle for his VP to use in his efforts to influence the culture of the affiliation would be as a member of the top management committee (the Management Policies Committee), and the VP set out to do that. In the committee's meetings he tried to exhibit a direct, to-the-point style of communicating, including challenging the thinking and decisions of the group or of individual members of the committee, including the two CEOs. This was not an unnatural thing for him to do, since his normal style involved such behavior anyway. However, in hindsight, this approach may have created at least three kinds of problems for him and his investment group. One problem was that he may have spent more time trying to influence the general affiliation culture during his first year or so in Madison than he did in trying to achieve a smooth integration of the two investment groups. A second problem is that he developed a reputation among people outside of his department as a "maverick" who was hard to get along with. This may have caused some to view his whole department in this way. The third problem concerned his style of implementing the "Century culture" within the investment function. This is a part of the story on which it will be useful to expand.

As we described in Chapter 3 when we were discussing perceived differences in the cultures of the two companies, many Century people felt that they had succeeded in developing a culture in which there was an expectation of superior performance. Century's CEO certainly felt this was the case and, in asking his investments VP to preserve and expand the Century culture within the affiliated group, he made it clear that the communication of and requirement for high levels of performance was a key aspect of his assignment. In addition, the VP had the perfect vehicle to do so. That is (as was pointed out in Chapter 7) he was expected to integrate the investment functions of the two companies, and this was going to require that he make some tough decisions concerning who among the management people from his own Century group and who from the CUNA Mutual group would become the management team of the combined department. He began this task by telling his people in Waverly that he wanted them all to make the move to Madison, but that he could not promise any of them that they would be members of his management team after the "shakeout." As we indicated earlier, all but one actually made the move, even without any guarantee. The VP did this in order to honor his promise to the CUNA Mutual people that he would not prejudge their levels of competence. He then waited nearly two years before establishing his final management team. However, during that period he conducted his typical (for him) performance reviews, which were very direct and critical, with all of his direct reports, including both the Century and the CUNA Mutual people. The Century people, most of whom had worked for him for some time were used to his style, but the CUNA Mutual people were not and some found his feedback very confrontational. He set about, during the subsequent two years, to help everyone on the staff make the improvements that he felt would be necessary for them to be considered legitimate candidates for the management team of the combined department. In spite of his efforts, it was natural that when he finally announced his management team, made up entirely of former Century people, there was resentment by at least some of the staff members.

We will discuss in Chapter 9 what lessons may be learned from this series of incidents and how some of these difficulties might have been avoided.

Top Management Integration

One of the most crucial, and most challenging, aspects of combining organizations concerns the integration of the top management of the involved companies. The affiliation of CUNA Mutual and Century Companies was no exception.

One of the reasons CUNA Mutual executives had originally become interested in Century Companies as a potential partner was because they felt that Century had some very capable management people who were experienced and knowledgable concerning the operation of an individual insurance business. Consequently, it was expected that at least some of the Century executives would become major players in the top management of the affiliated group. This, of course, was the case. It had begun, as we have described, with the appointment of Century's VP of investments as head of the investment function and as a member of the Management Policies Committee. In addition, Century's COO was later named head of Individual Insurance Operations for the affiliated group and a member of the Management Policies Committee. Century's VP of Marketing was originally named to head the joint venture, Plan America, and later became head of all of the affiliated group's individual marketing systems, including face-to-face, direct-mail, and telemarketing. These appointments resulted in a truly integrated top management group, since, along with the above- named Century people, CUNA Mutual people made up the rest of the top group, including their chief legal counsel who headed the legal function, and other

CUNA Mutual executives who were appointed to head the IS function, the marketing function, and the Corporate Staff Group. This, of course, leaves the question of the very top job, and it is this position which has created the most difficulty.

When the companies originally came together, Century's CEO had in mind that he and the CUNA Mutual CEO would retire at the same time and that it would be their joint task to put in place a succession plan that would ensure that their combined companies would be well led. As discussed earlier, to set the stage, each became "deputy CEO" of the other company. Century's CEO began to spend two days a week in his Madison office. CUNA Mutual's CEO spent far less time in Waverly because of his travel schedule, but occasionally attended executive meetings and made appearances on some important occasions. Century's CEO continued to push to establish a clear plan for succession and dates-certain for both his and his counterpart's retirements. However the CUNA Mutual CEO showed less interest in such matters, and finally the Century head established a group consisting of himself and three consultants who knew the companies well and in whom he had confidence, to engage in a process of determining the competencies necessary in the top jobs for the affiliated group. In addition, he succeeded in getting members of the Affiliation Steering Committee of the board of directors of the affiliated group involved as an oversight body to insure that an orderly process be undertaken to establish a succession plan. With the key pieces of the puzzle in place, he felt secure in the knowledge that he had done what he could to ensure the future of his company. He retired in March 1993. The Century COO was named president of Century Companies and the CUNA Mutual CEO became CEO of the affiliated group, including Century Companies. Century's chief financial officer became COO of Century Companies. Even with all of these transition steps, the Century CEO's retirement was a very significant event to many of his people, and it was made even more so since it took place while details of the affiliation were still being worked out. Because he knew this would be true, he desired to minimize the impact of it, and he chose the "normal" retirement time, that is age sixty-five, to do so. He made the decision in January 1992 and he informed the Century board at that time. However, the public announcement was made in the summer of 1992.

Then, in March 1994, the CUNA Mutual and Century Life boards of directors announced that it was the intention of the CEO of the two companies to retire. No specific retirement date was set. Rather it was announced that the CEO would, "await the selection and installation of his successor and work with the appointee at the pleasure of the board to insure a smooth and orderly transition." The board established a succession committee, and indicated that the search process would be, "an open one with the objective of the committee to find the best possible candidate for the position." The committee then retained the services of an executive search firm and began a wide-ranging search for a new CEO. Candidates from within the affiliated companies, from outside the companies but within the Credit Union Movement, and from outside the Credit Union Movement were considered. Early in 1995, the head of the CUNA Mutual Insurance Society of Canada was selected as the new CEO. He took over his new responsibilities on March 1, 1995.

Integration of the Boards of Directors

In Chapter 7, we described the plan for integrating the two companies' boards of directors, as well as the early steps taken to implement that plan. In this chapter, we want to include some more recent changes in the combined board and point out the implications of those changes for the affiliation.

When the president and CEO of Century retired, he also stepped down from his position on the board of directors. He was replaced by a gentleman who had been a consultant to Century and who had a long background in the management of career agency systems. This was intended to send a signal to Century's career system people that they would, even in their CEO's absence, have a knowledgable and sympathetic ear on the board. It may be of interest to note that when the Century CEO retired, some board members expressed an interest in having him continue on as a member of the board. He, however, decided not to do so because he felt that there was too much of that, retired executives being retained in "consultant" roles, going on in the industry and so his involvement with the affiliation came to an abrupt end in March 1993. Another, and very significant, development occurred on June 20, 1993 when the former chairman of the Century board (before the affiliation) was elected secretary of the board of the CUNA Mutual Insurance Group. The immediate past chairman of the CUNA Mutual Board acknowledged this decision as, "an example of the bonding that is occurring among the directors and the great respect the directors have for one another to make things happen for the affiliated companies." The election of the former Century chairman to the secretary's post is of particular significance because the normal progression on the CUNA Mutual board is that one moves, in two-year terms, from secretary, to treasurer, to vicechairman to chairman. If this pattern is followed, he would become chairman of the board of the CUNA Mutual Insurance Group late in the 1990s. If the reader will recall how much of the early part of our story concerned CUNA Mutual's protectiveness of its market, it may become clear what a momentous event that will be. The fact that the early steps have been taken that may result in such an occurrence really does, as CUNA Mutual's past board chairman said, indicate a great deal of respect and, we would add, a great deal of trust.

We turn now to our final chapter in which we will bring together what we feel has been learned from this experience. It has been our objective in this book to tell an interesting and informative story, but we also want to make explicit some of the lessons we have learned that may make the path smoother for others to follow.

9

Lessons Learned

As we pointed out in Chapter 1, the results after five years of the affiliation between CUNA Mutual and Century have, for the most part, exceeded expectations. However, in any innovative venture there are bound to be lessons learned. In this chapter we will summarize for the reader what has been learned from this experience. We have organized these lessons into five categories: strategic issues, cultural issues, communications issues, transformation issues, and additional issues.

STRATEGIC ISSUES

The most important issue is, of course, to make sure your strategic focus is well defined and visible throughout the process. We have three lessons for your consideration.

Lesson One: Keep Strategy Ahead of Structure

One of the reasons that so many mergers fail to reach their objectives is that they get this turned around and allow structure to precede strategy. There is a tendency to lose sight of their strategic objectives and turn the merger process over to the legal and financial staffs. In the case of the affiliation, the primary vehicle to build a sustainable strategy was the Plan America system discussed in Chapters 6 and 7. Even moving the blocks of business to communities of interest to achieve greater critical mass was secondary to the Plan America objective.

In Chapter 7 we discussed the integration of the legal and investment function. The integration of these two functions would be typical of the process used in a merger. In the affiliation those two functions were integrated while the companies were pursuing the Plan America plan and moving the blocks of business. That was done because these functions were "stand-alone labor intensive" functions, and it was done based on the integration discipline described in Chapter 7. The bottom line indicated, however, that the integration of these two functions would result in annual savings of less than $1 million whereas in moving blocks of business and the Plan America marketing plan many millions of dollars were involved. There probably is a natural tendency when consolidating functions in mergers to say, "this is something more tangible—I can deal with it," and to lose sight of the strategy. Obviously, organizations also have a tendency to address issues about which individuals in the organizations have the greatest day-to-day concerns. However, as indicated later in these lessons, it is necessary to have a discipline to monitor the strategy that is to be followed.

There may be another way to look at this issue. CUNA Mutual and Century, in the very early stages of their discussions, had talked about merger but, as indicated in Chapter 5, had decided against that idea. It is possible at some time in the future a merger could become a reality but by the time that would happen it would be a "nonevent" since the companies would have focused so intensely on their strategy for so long and would have become recognized as one and the same in the market-place. Thus it was understood that if a merger occured and it was an "event" it would imply that the companies were taking their focus off of the strategy and getting structure ahead of its rightful place.

The full potential of expected synergies will be missed if the focus becomes the mechanics of the structure. Staffs will be skeptical, and it will be impossible to satisfy all of their concerns while talking about strategies because it will remain unclear how this will specifically affect every individual. Even in the face of pressure to be more specific, it is important to avoid caving in because those issues, while important to individuals, are not central to the strategy. Imagine a leader taking a group of people across a steep arching bridge over a river. The leader knows that the bridge is attached to the opposite shore or it would collapse but it is impossible to know exactly what it looks like on the other side. The leader must keep telling the people, "I'm a little further ahead than you are; I can't yet see the end; you and I know we must cross to the other side; I know this bridge is attached and every time I get more insight of what it looks like ahead I will tell you." The leader needs to continue to earn the group's trust and keep focused on the strategy in order to maximize the potential for all concerned.

Lesson Two: Develop a Well-thought-out Integration Strategy

It will, of course, be necessary to develop a plan for integrating the organizations because as the strategy discussed above is pursued, there will be obvious synergies to be gained as the strategic plan evolves. This plan must be thorough, fair, and focused on the best utilization of human resources available. There are two major steps to this process, namely, (1) how to sort out the roles or accountabilities each party will assume and (2) matching the individual with the best potential to the job requirements.

In step 1 it is important to do more than simply lay out a job description for a particular role. It is necessary to get the respective counterparts from the two companies together with a disinterested third party to sort out the accountabilities.

The best results were achieved with a minimum of anxiety in the affiliation where the respective functions from the two companies used an organizational specialist for the third party. This process, described at the end of Chapter 7, was one in which the net result was an understanding of who had the principal accountabilties, who played a secondary role or that there was to be an equally shared responsibility.

There was an example in the affiliation in integrating human resources which illustrated the merits of this approach. The Madison human resources department had sent a memo to the Waverly human resources department regarding a particular matter. The head of the Waverly human resources group realized that the memo was inconsistent with what had been agreed to in sorting out accountabilities. Instead of having to go "to the mat" to resolve the issue, he simply referred in a phone call to their memo regarding responsibilities and within minutes the misunderstanding was resolved. Early clarification of respective roles is essential and reviewing the principal accountabilities is an effective tool to reduce anxiety and enhance productivity which in the final analysis helps the organization keep its focus on the affiliation strategy.

In step 2 matching individual capacity with job requirements was essential in making the most of the affiliation. A disciplined, objective process will in the final analysis enhance the productivity of the staff because it will become apparent that the organizations are doing the best they can to serve the customer. The process used in the affiliation was described in Chapter 7. It was conceived at a meeting of the board ad hoc committees in Chicago early in the affiliation process. In summary the process (1) defines the requirements of the job, not only at the time but in the subsequent five years, (2) reviews potential candidates through performance appraisals, psychological assessments, and behavioral analysis for potential developmental capacity, and, (3) conducts a type of "player draft" to match individual capacity with the job responsibilities. Obviously this approach is not a pure science. You have to use good judgment but the discipline will help you avoid significant pitfalls and putting individuals in positions which are beyond their capacity to perform. It is much better to use background data plus good judgment than to rely on intuition.

Lesson Three: Develop a Plan so that the Entire Organization Will Keep a Focus on Your Primary Strategy

For the affiliation the primary long-term sustainable strategy was Plan America. It was hard to keep the organizations focused on that issue. As reported in other literature there is a tendency to focus on mechanics and operational issues, whereas it is understandably more difficult to think about marketing and making new things happen. While it is easier to "count" and to deal with hands-on issues, they tend to be short term. In the case of Plan America, for example, when the individual who was to head up this new marketing project arrived in Madison, it seemed as if he was not expected in that there was no desk, secretary, assigned space, or anything else that would indicate the organization was prepared to support his efforts. In retrospect it would have been better if the companies had designated a place for this new operation as an integral part of the marketing operation in Madison rather than simply finding space somewhere in the building. Plan America was the primary strategic thrust of the affiliation, and it would probably have benefited by having the support of the entire marketing structure. Furthermore, all support staff located in Madison and Waverly should have been centralized in this new space to facilitate the project, even though this would have meant adding excess staff in the short term.

A different approach was used in the case of the movement of the blocks of business from Michigan to Waverly, Iowa. A separate building was used for all of the new business that was moved with the understanding that initially it would involve excess staff. This separate location made sense because this was something of a "stand-alone" operation and it also gave the staff an opportunity to work out the kinks in the process and to make sure that the company maintained service to the customer. Eventually it is intended that this separate operation will probably be integrated with the rest of the organization to realize greater efficiencies. While this proved to be a desirable move in the affiliation it is another example of how corporations tend to do a better job with operations issues than with marketing projects.

The strategic thrust, as difficult as it is, needs to be monitored to expectations on at least a monthly basis and to be discussed with the entire senior staff and board to maintain necessary visibility.

CULTURAL ISSUES

It is important that anyone who embarks on combining companies, be it merger, joint venture, or some type of affiliation, have an appreciation for the difference in cultures between the two companies. The lessons we learned in the affiliation follow.

Lesson Four: Understand the Difference in Corporate Cultures and Define What Type of Culture You Want to Create

In Chapter 6 we discussed initial attempts at group interaction among the companies' senior staffs to help them get to know each other better and, in particular, to help them develop a greater appreciation for each others' cultures. In addition, Century scheduled several bus trips to Madison where all associates could visit the site of the other company. To demonstrate involvement in this process the CEO of Century flew back to Waverly from Madison in order to be a part of that process and involved with all the staff. While these meetings were productive, it would have been desirable to go beyond these meetings.

The suggestion would be for senior management to achieve not only an understanding of the differences in culture but to jointly define the cultural characteristics they want to foster in the combined organizations. Dialogue should then be held with other levels of management so there is an understanding of how the organization should function. Monthly meetings should be held with the senior management to assess what progress is being made toward the objective and to discuss examples to help clarify the objective. Human resource staff should be used to facilitate defining the cultural objective and monitoring of progress. Note the discussion of this type of approach under lesson 23, on creating a "transparent" organization.

Lesson Five: Develop a Method to Work Through Differences in Culture

The reader may feel that this has already been covered but it deserves special focus. Studies show that most executives do not take explicit account of culture differences in making integration decisions. In the affiliation, because the obvious long-term benefits were good for both organizations, there was a tendency to downplay any cultural differences.

One of CUNA Mutual's key strengths was the extent to which they had become market driven, whereas one of Century's key strengths was how they had become process driven. Each strength was a plus to the synergy of the combination of the two companies. At the same time each company sometimes became impatient with the other company's strength. That is, CUNA Mutual believed that there were times that Century took too long to work through an issue and conversely Century thought that it appeared too easy for the market to dictate to CUNA Mutual.

In human beings a strength, if overdone (think in terms of turning up the volume on a radio), can become a weakness. The same is true of organizations. If CUNA Mutual, for example, bends over too far in yielding to the demands of the credit union, it becomes a drag on the organization. On the other hand, if Century becomes too focused on the process they can become paralyzed by the analysis and fail to respond to the market in a timely fashion. Each company, in fact, needed the strength of the other and the combination of the two enhanced both organizations.

As suggested in one of the later lessons, the companies should appoint a transition director, (probably one of the CEOs), but one member of the high level transition team should also be an outsider who has no previous ties to either company. That individual should be involved full time during the transition to act as a type of conscience as the companies move through the change. If at any point, a strength is tending to become a weakness, it would be his or her responsibility to point this out to the transition director.

As indicated in a previous lesson, the differences in culture should be thoroughly discussed up front so there is a clear understanding of the differences and a resolution as to the type of culture that the combined companies should represent. Hypothetical situations could be used to illustrate the differences and how you would resolve these differences as they surface. During the transition, resolution of differences should be reported monthly to senior officers and to directors. This process will help the affiliation move very deliberately toward the desired culture and reduce some of the frustration organizations experience when cultures tend to clash.

COMMUNICATION ISSUES

It is very critical to spend a great deal of time thinking through all of the communications issues. The lessons we learned follow.

Lesson Six: Plan and Orchestrate Communications Carefully

There are three essential steps in developing the communications plan: (a) develop a set of SOCOs, (b) assemble a team to lay out the plan, and (c) outline who needs to know what and when.

The main goal of step a is to develop a set of SOCOs. SOCO stands for Single Overriding Communications Objective. It is critical that you define at the outset what three to six key points you are trying to make to your particular public. While the SOCOs will essentially be the same for each public you are dealing with, the priority and importance may differ. Think in terms of who you are talking to and what are their concerns. It would be advisable to tell your audience at the outset what you are going to tell them, give them the details, and then summarize and end with your SOCOs.

In step b, as the CEO, surround yourself with three individuals who will lay out the plan. Use the head of your human resource function and your public relations function because of their ability to communicate and because they may have a better understanding of what the particular public concerns are that you are trying to address. In addition it would be helpful to have those two individuals work with the individual who is closest to the CEO and understands the CEO's thinking and concerns. These three individuals together with the CEO should at the outset agree on the SOCOs.

In step c, the plan should be fine-tuned to cover who needs to know what and when. The plan should include both internal and external publics. By carefully triggering the order of the communications plan and implementing promptly, anxiety and rumors will be reduced. Managers, for example, should know before staff because they may have a different set of questions and would be in a position to answer questions from staff members when they receive the information. Staff members should receive the communications before the plan is communicated to the general public so that they would be "in the know" before the neighbors. This seems like a self evident suggestion but the detailed plan suggested is often ignored in business. Consistency in this approach will develop a culture in which the staff feels well informed and will be in a position to dispel rumors because they will feel that they will always "know when they should know" and everything else is just that—rumor.

Lesson Seven: Do Not Delay Passing on Information

Previous authors have suggested that the implementation of action steps involved in combining organizations should be undertaken at the earliest reasonable time. In Tichy's 1993 book describing Jack Welch's approach to changing General Electric, he suggests a three-stage process followed by Welch. In the first stage, which Tichy called the "awareness" stage, Welch made a statement about the future by significantly downsizing the organization. The second step was to establish the vision and, step three was to follow through with the implementation. Such an approach would have been more radical and too simplistic in the CUNA Mutual and Century affiliation.

A great deal of time elapsed between the "selling" of the benefits of the affiliation and the time at which the staff of either company could actually begin to see the benefits. As far as home office staff was concerned the design/build concept described in Chapters 6 and 7 produced some early benefits for the staff in Waverly in that the transfer of business meant more jobs for a group of people who had experienced several reductions in staff. In Madison, there was a transfer of work to Waverly but the resulting excess staff in Madison were given other opportunities within the organization. The most significant problem caused by the delays was to the Century career agents. Access to a sponsored market, which was a solution to the perennial problem for life insurance agents, referred leads, was taking too long to implement. This led to significant distrust, unrest, reduced productivity, and even defections among members of the field force.

In the insurance industry, perhaps more than in any other business, one needs to consider the differences among "subcultures" within the organization. The members of the distribution systems in the insurance industry are usually more independent and entrepreneurial than are the home office staff people. The proximity of the home office staff, the ability to respond to concerns, and the fact that work opportunities were limited in the economy made it easier to control the dissemination of information and therefore achieve the desirable results. The independence and the dispersion of the field force made it more difficult. Furthermore the normal first step for most companies to improve their bottom line is to cut expenses. Century had done that within the office and to the field force that would mean cutting commissions. In addition the industry was hurting for production, and it was easy for the insurance agent to not only switch his new business to another company but also be tempted to take business already written and transfer it to the new company, especially since the new company would also pay commissions on the old business transferred. Furthermore, because of the turmoil in the industry there had been some cases in companies where changes had been mismanaged resulting in a "run" on the company to the point where the State Insurance Commissioner had stepped in to prevent insolvency. The entire home office management staff at Century had been through a series of survey feedback sessions on creating a climate for performance and were fully aware of the issues the company faced and knew that senior management had no alternative but to act or risk losing their ability to lead. The Century field force was not in the same position of understanding.

There is merit in being sensitive to the membership that you are trying to lead but that strength, if overdone, becomes a weakness. You can not afford to wait to initiate change until it starts "raining" and once you start the process you must keep up the momentum. Do not delay the process, but be sensitive to the culture within the organization or within subgroups of the organization. In effect, you must walk a fine line. You want to demonstrate feelings and compassion but being overly concerned about feelings could hurt the momentum. There are some who will always say "don't do it" or will never grasp the rationale but you need to keep in mind your motives and why you are making the changes. It is crucial to keep in mind that, in pursuing a strategy to build a sustainable future, structural decisions such as where a function should be located, must remain secondary to the strategic objective of building a future that will provide jobs and opportunities for many individuals. A suggested approach with any group would be as follows:

a. Assign a half dozen members of the group to work with management in the implementation. Their purpose would be to critique the process and at the same time act as ambassadors to help clarify areas where they detect misunderstanding.

b. Approach the process in three stages: (1) describe the concerns to the membership, (2) repeat the concerns and lay out the options to be considered, and (3) spell out the vision and the implementation steps.

c. Send a consistent, open, honest, and strong message to the staff that change is necessary, and it will happen. To control your destiny you must become a part of the solution, not the problem.

Lesson Eight: Do Not Oversell the Change

Century management was convinced that the affiliation was good for the career system. They knew that this would certainly be true in the long term. However, they failed to realize how difficult it would be to enter the Credit Union market. They did not appreciate that CUNA Mutual did not "own" the credit unions. At the same time, Century management realized that the most direct contact with the policyholders, who had to approve the affiliation, was the distribution system and therefore management needed the support of the agents. It should also be understood that the field managers, who were concerned about where they would end up in the affiliation, were ambivalent about directing the focus of the agents.

In part as a result of the way they are usually compensated, insurance agents have traditionally been more concerned about results in the short term (that is, how any given change might affect their productivity this year) than over the long term. Lead generation had been an industry problem, and the affiliation appeared to address that problem. However, when agents receive leads in their business they expect to be able to call on their new contacts immediately and, in the case of the affiliation, that did not turn out to be possible.

Another element that worked against the agents was the question in their minds as to whether Century was giving up on the career distribution system. The cost problems the industry was having with traditional distribution systems were well known and Century had already experimented with a number of alternatives. In addition, it was a field perception that an inordinate proportion of the company's resources was being spent on this one venture. This created a lot of anxiety about their future with Century.

While the Century management never intended to oversell the benefits of the affiliation the combination of the above resulted in an overenthusiastic presentation by management and unrealistic expectations on the part of the agents. Many agents came away from early meetings expecting to be able to go back to their agencies, receive a list of prospects from credit unions in their areas, and simply fill in their appointment books. It turned out to be a bit more complicated than that. The integration of the affiliated group's distribution systems eventually took place (see Chapter 8), but it took much longer than the agents had originally expected.

Our suggestions are:

a. Make a concerted effort to understand the dynamics and expectations of subcultures in your organization.
b. Use several members of the group to critique communications and to support the effort.
c. Be open and honest in describing both the long- and short-term benefits and risks of any change.

Lesson Nine: Do Not Withhold Information Longer Than Necessary

If put in the positive, this lesson would be "tell your people everything you can, as soon as you can." Almost all of the sources we cited in Chapter 2 that offered guidelines for successfully combining organizations included this suggestion in one form or another. Withholding information almost always leads to excessive rumormongering and the rumors are almost never positive.

The Century CEO at times received criticism from within the organization during the affiliation process suggesting that he was withholding information or that he was not telling them everything he knew. This could be expected in a "transparent organization" (see Lesson 23), but again we need to take a look at the subgroups within the culture and try to understand their expectations. Century worked hard at treating everyone in the organization as equals but the reader needs to consider a "need- to-know" policy within the context of the notion of "full business partners." In this context the board of directors of Century were full business partners and had a "need to know" all of the issues under consideration. Full business partners never make decisions for their partners. The reader needs to understand that we are discussing here the combination of two mutual companies and not stock companies. While it is apparent that not every mutual company functions this way, the true charter for every mutual board is, to the best of their ability, to represent the policyholders and not their personal agendas or that of the CEO.

In the case of the field force or the home office staff, in this sense, they are not full partners. There are certain decisions, particularly in the area of corporate governance and strategy that a CEO is expected to make with board partners on behalf of the policyholders. The CEO would be shirking his or her responsibility if such issues were to be put to a vote within the internal operation. Again we need to look at the expectations of the subcultures.

A specific issue of corporate governance that arose in the affiliation may help clarify this particular point. The bottom line of the affiliation was that Century had the business expertise in the individual market and CUNA Mutual had the market. Obviously it was going to take more than simply good faith for Century to gain access to the market. As explained in Chapter 7, the resolution to this issue was for CUNA Mutual to have six members on the Century board and for Century to retain five members. Clearly this was an issue to be resolved at the board level. As "partners" the board members looked at the issue in terms of what was best for the policyholders that they represented and not their personal agendas.

To the home office staff this was obviously a piece of information that needed to be dealt with in order for them to understand the basis for the decision and the benefits. Clearly they did not "need to know" before the fact to fulfill their functions in the organization but at the same time, in an open and honest organization the information would be shared but after the fact. The view of the board in the organization was that they were seen as supportive and not adversarial. While reports and discussions of issues were held with the board, management never reported back to the staff what the board said. In this environment there was little interest on the part of most home office staff people in what went on at board meetings except if there was a specific issue that involved them and was reported by them to the board.

The perception and the expectation by the field force was different than the home office. There have been cases in the industry where agents were asked to serve on the board in an attempt to stimulate the cohesiveness of the organization and encourage agents' enthusiasm for the organization. As indicated earlier, many insurance agents are more independent than home office staff and feel they are not beholden to management and are truly in control of their own destinies. Therefore, their perception is that what goes on at board meetings has a very direct bearing on their future, and they need to get close to that action. The Century CEO had at least two agents suggest that they felt they had the qualifications to serve on the Century board. That type of suggestion would never come from a home office staff member. Again, in terms of good corporate governance you need to have policyholder representation and not individuals who would have a personal conflict of interest. The point is that the field force had a different perception of what goes on at board meetings than did the home office and felt they had a greater vested interest. Thus because of these perceptions, the issue of board control would be of greater concern to the field force than it would be to the home office. Clearly the field force did not "need to know" this information to continue to serve the policyholders and to perform their role in the company. But management should have taken greater care and been more deliberate in explaining the rationale for this decision after the fact.

Prior to the discussions that took place between the two CEOs, it had become apparent to the Century CEO (through his own analysis and through extensive discussions with experts in the business) that the form any truly workable solution to the Century cost dilemma would probably take would involve a more extensive set of changes than most, if not all, of his people (and, for that matter, board members also) would be comfortable with. Consequently, he undertook a rather long-term program of slowly helping them to become aware of the realities in their industry in general (see Chapter 4) and the particular issues of Century Companies' situation (see Chapter 3) so that they would realize, as he did, that the option of remaining competitive as a small midwestern mutual was not realistic. Furthermore, later on, when his early discussions with the CUNA Mutual CEO were underway, he, once again, consciously withheld from his people a full disclosure concerning the nature of the probable form the affiliation would take because he wanted to avoid overwhelming them and because there was not yet a "need to know." As we look back now, he may have been overcautious, or we might say he underestimated his people's capacity to handle change, but we might also speculate that the affiliation may never have come to pass if he had behaved differently. (See Chapter 5 for examples of people's reactions to this process.)

The lesson, however, remains to disclose information as soon as possible to reduce anxiety in the organization and to facilitate the continued focus on the mission of the company.

Lesson Ten: Do Not Make Promises You Cannot Keep

When organizations change, there may be a tendency on the part of management to make promises that will help enlist the support of staff and to take the heat off of management and to avoid confrontation, (Mirvis & Marks, 1992a; Pritchett, 1985).

When it was decided to integrate the investment operations in Madison early in the affiliation, the new senior investment officer for the affiliation encouraged his (Waverly) staff to follow him with literally *no* promises. At the time they moved to Madison they did not know if they would, in the long term, have a job. Only one staff member chose to leave the company instead of moving to Madison. This is probably an extreme example of the lesson of not making any promises. In retrospect it might have been better to have the senior officer move back and forth between the two locations until definite assignments could have been made. In the meantime, the staff would had to have been told what was happening, and been asked to keep doing the jobs they were doing and told that as soon as it was possible, job assignments would be made. This situation was, however, very unusual. The company was anxious to initiate its design/build form of affiliation and the integration of the investment unit was the first opportunity to illustrate that the companies were serious about the affiliation. In addition, it would be fair to point out that the Waverly staff had experienced intense training and development over the preceding ten years and there was thus a high probability that they would be retained. The development of the staff was a result of an "investment physical" that had been done in the early 1980s. (See Lesson 23.)

By way of contrast, as far as the agency field force was concerned there was a tendency, as described above, to oversell the immediate benefits.   The companies tended to describe all the ways that the field force would benefit and the problem was that the plan was "rolled out" over a period of four or five years. This delay developed an air of mistrust. When the marketing plan was finally rolled out they did a much better job by advising those individuals who would not have a similar job in the new organization before any public meetings so there would be no unrealistic expectations. Furthermore, in the public meetings they advised the group as to what decisions had been made, and what choices people would have, telling them that not everyone would have a new assignment. This, of course, resulted in some anxiety but they were told to do the best job they could where they were in order to be considered for new opportunities.

Three agency managers left the organization before the marketing plan was rolled out and took some of their agents with them. When the companies were more direct as in the roll out of the marketing plan it was estimated that twenty agents and one manager decided to leave.

The lesson again is do not make promises you cannot keep simply to keep the heat off.

Lesson Eleven: Be Acutely Aware of Your Comments

Be sensitive to the fact that even casual comments by top managerment can have a significant impact. This has also been suggested by other authors (Pritchett, 1985). It was obvious to all staff members that the industry was going through traumatic change. If there is general ambiguity and little information people tend to read into issues that something big is about to happen. The CEO of CUNA Mutual happened to mention that he was having lunch with the CEO of Century. This was only their second meeting and in spite of the fact that they were at an industry meeting where there were a lot of CEOs, the staff who heard this comment assumed that something big was about to happen.

The CEO of Century tells the story of one evening when he was working late he happened to mention to the cleaning help after leaving the washroom, that the soap dispenser was not functioning very well. That word was passed on to the staff and the next day maintenance dropped what ever else they were doing to make sure that the soap dispenser was changed before the end of the day; and that was under normal circumstances. With an industry in upheaval it is as if the "antenna" of every staff member is turned up and they will put their own "spin" on comment they hear which naturally will become magnified.

TRANSFORMATION ISSUES

Following is a list of lessons that we learned concerning the actual process of organizational combination.

Lesson Twelve: Appoint a Transformation Director

Many writings suggest that you "track" the progress of the combination carefully (Mirvis & Marks, 1992b). Formal tracking of various components of the combination allows management to know whether the transition is proceeding according to plan or veering off course and to identify "hotspots" before they flare out of control. This kind of tracking also enhances upward communication and highlights the need for midcourse corrections. "Tracking" tends to imply number crunching in monitoring progress. We are suggesting to the reader that you go beyond simply "tracking." The role needs to be more proactive and to keeping a constant focus on the strategy, anticipating problems, and making course corrections in advance.

The affiliation agreement between CUNA Mutual and Century contained a mechanism for resolving problems should they arise. At the same time they had an attitude that if they had to resort to the affiliation document to resolve a problem they were probably in trouble. While in the long run it worked out, they could have saved time, reduced anxiety, and improved productivity sooner if they had developed a better tracking system for the affiliation as a whole. In the marketing operation they did, over a period of several years, develop a tracking system to monitor results and move the operation toward the vision.

Our suggestion to improve results was touched on in Lesson One above, that is, keeping strategy ahead of structure. The experience of the affiliation also suggests that one of the CEOs be named the transformation director and that on this person's staff there be a number cruncher for "tracking," but, in addition, there should be an up-front understanding of what you are trying to do and reports made to the senior staff at least monthly and to the board quarterly. Progress should be measured against specific benchmarks. It would be advisable to have a disinterested third party on this high level transition team to help maintain objectivity and keep the focus on the basic strategy.

It would be desirable to have the office of the transformation director separated from those of the combined organization's top management. As indicated previously, the Century CEO delegated the primary role of managing the Century operation to a COO. At the same time he spent three to four days a week in Madison. However, he had an office in Madison in "executive row" and that tended to carry the implication that he was focused on management of the operation instead of on the affiliation. In many respects that was, in fact, how the role played out. Also, as indicated earlier, each CEO had been named Deputy CEO of the other company. While that had some visible implications that were helpful it probably was done more to placate the egos of the CEOs. The point here is that perception does become reality, and one can tend to lose sight of the basic strategic objective, again because it is easier to deal with the mechanics.

The role of the transformation director would be more of a problem identification responsibility, facilitating solutions and being, in effect, the guardian of the strategy.

Lesson Thirteen: Senior Management Should Keep Hands-on During the Change Process

While there is a need to delegate in order to involve staff that are crucial in supporting the plan, there is also, in many change efforts, a tendency to "undermanage" the process. When the affiliation process was started, the CEO from Century established the role of COO in Waverly and took the investment officer and the marketing officer to Madison. The investment officer worked on combining the investment operations from the two companies and the marketing officer focused on the new marketing plan. The CEO started to spend three to four days a week in Madison. As far as the Century operation was concerned that worked fine.

Because the Madison operation was not a singular line of business as was Century, the CUNA Mutual staff were very involved in many projects. As a result, the presence of the Century CEO in Madison was viewed more as an extension of all the things that were already being done. The focus on the key strategy of the affiliation in particular was diminished. It was several years after the Plan America project had begun that the board, through a focused seminar, and the CUNA Mutual staff, because of the results that were being achieved while the rest of the business was very flat, realized how significant this project was going to be to their future.

It would be our suggestion that, through a role negotiation process between the CEOs, a clear set of "expectations" be established at the outset and then regularly monitored. Organizational combinations need someone involved with hands-on who has the whole picture of what the organizations are trying to accomplish. In the affiliation only a few part-time people were designated to support the Century CEO in Madison. It would have been better if a full-time staff of three or four had supported the CEO in monitoring the results of the affiliation. It takes this type of effort to continue to hold up the strategic objective flag and avoid letting structural issues dictate progress. In the affiliation, the positioning of the CEO of Century in Madison probably was viewed more as a structural assignment than as a focus on the key strategy. Several of the sources we reviewed agreed that most transformation and combinations within companies are "under-managed (Mirvis & Marks, 1992a). Once again, this guideline should not be taken completely at face value. Several of our experiences, as well as several of the sources we reviewed led us to conclude that it is important to delegate significant portions of the combination activity to staff whose support is crucial. It is probable that both sides of this issue are important, which means that top management must walk a line between undermanaging or abdicating on the one hand and shutting people out on the other. The prescription is probably something like this. Form lots of high involvement transition teams and have them actively involved in substantive pieces of the combination process and then remain highly visible, cheer-lead, intervene when they seem to need your help, get them resources they need, keep the vision clear to them, and so on, (Hammer & Champy, 1993).

Lesson Fourteen: Clarify the Role of the Consultant

It has been suggested several times in the lessons above that you use a third party to help in the process. Not only would a particular expertise be helpful but a disinterested party would add objectivity to the process. Obviously you need someone in the organization to drive the process but a neutral party would add credibility and expedite the project.

You need to make sure, however, that you are not delegating the total process to the neutral party. The productivity of the consultant is directly related to the capacity of the individual (the transformation director) within the organization to perform. The consultant must have the objective of transferring his or her capacity to the organization and in effect working himself or herself out of a job.

Lesson Fifteen: Do Not Use the Most Extreme Example of Your Culture as Your Cultural Change Agent

In some of the lessons above, we talked about the importance of developing an understanding up front of the culture that you want to achieve. In the affiliation, members of management had discussed perceptions each organization had of the other, but the next step of agreeing on what they wanted to achieve was not taken. We have suggested that not only do you want to agree as to what you want to achieve but that you need to have a process to monitor your progress in moving toward your objective.

In the CUNA Mutual and Century affiliation, the Century chief investment officer was asked to play the role of cultural change agent in addition to his reponsibility of integrating the investment operations.   In retrospect, this was probably not a reasonable assignment. However, at the same time if you have a consensus up front as to what you are trying to achieve it will make it easier for any change agent. In the case of the affiliation there were desirable cultural aspects of each of the organizations that needed to be preserved and while, as time passes, the organizations appear to be moving in that direction, a more conscious process would have been healthier for the organizations. In some environments there have been instances in which especially radical change agents have been "chewed up and spit out" by the organization because the individual has few allies. In the case of the affiliation, that did not happen, because from the board on down, the organizations were determined to make the affiliation work because of the benefits that would inure to the policyholders.

Furthermore, it probably is too much to ask of any one individual to be the focal point for change and when you do point to examples of change be sure you use your best resource who is also politically sensitive.

Lesson Sixteen: Have a Technique for Counterparts in the Organizations to Become Better Acquainted

This process should start with the CEOs. It is our suggestion that, in the case of the CEOs in particular, you use a psychological consultant to develop a profile of each individual in terms of basic values and human behavior in order for each individual to have a better understanding of the others prior to beginning to work together. In the case of the affiliation the CEOs proceeded on good faith and simply developed a set of job descriptions to be used as a structure for their relationship. But it needs to go beyond that into a type of role negotiation in which the parties identify what they want and need from each other in terms of behavior and patterns of interaction.

It has been well documented that the reason many mergers are aborted or that the average life of a joint venture is less than three years is because the egos of the CEOs or board members get in the way. Certainly in the case of the affiliation it would have been a travesty if the effort had been terminated because of egos, because the ultimate result was extremely beneficial to the policyholders. But greater and faster progress would have been made and a healthier example would have been set for the rest of the organization if the CEOs had developed a more explicit "psychological contract" early on.

In addition to going through role negotiation, it might have been helpful if, after the roles had been defined, a monitoring process would have been put in place. The affiliation board ad hoc committees had retained outside experts to look over their shoulders as they moved through the process. It would have been desirable if they had jointly selected a third party to meet monthly with the CEOs and then report to the joint ad hoc committees at least on a quarterly basis. This might help to assure that all the issues stay on the table and that the focus of everyone remains on the strategic goals.

A similar process should be used below the level of the CEO. In the affiliation there was a lot of interaction between counterparts that was voluntarily initiated. This was healthy but there were instances where one or the other assumed that in the end there would be some type of consolidation and he or she would be picked to lead the group. This caused some anxiety and some direct confrontation which could have been minimized or avoided. Instead of the Board a committee of senior management could have been assigned the task of monitoring the progress. Such a committee was established in the affiliation but it met only if a crisis arose whereas it should have met on a regular basis to monitor progress patterned after an example set by the CEOs.

Lesson Seventeen: Involve HR Staff on the High Level Transition Team

Involve human resource (HR) executives from both companies in early dealings and get their counsel not only on human resource department matters but more broadly on the human implications of the combination. This has been suggested by other authors as well (Mirvis & Marks, 1992a). This was not done as well as it could have been done in the affiliation. The work that was done in investments, marketing, financial, and information systems within functions could have gone much smoother with an HR specialist as a type of consultant to the senior executive of the particular functions as they were accomplishing the transition.

If the senior Human Resource officer does not report directly to the CEO under normal circumstances he or she should do so for the purposes of the transition. Obviously the CEO has to have confidence in the HR officer but it helps to keep staff sensitivities at a high level during traumatic change and if changes are to be implemented such as in job descriptions, definition of principal accountabilities, interrelation of accountabilities, evaluation of staff, and so forth, it is helpful to have the best knowledge of these issues on hand to expedite the follow through which reduces anxiety within the office.

ADDITIONAL ISSUES

Some important additional lessons learned follow.

Lesson Eighteen: The CEO Must Focus on Board Integration Early in the Process

All of the current literature points to the fact that there will be further consolidation in the financial services industry especially for medium and smaller companies. Normally companies tend to wait until their financials have reached the critical stage before they take action. Obviously before you make any strategic moves you need the blessing of the company board. It is helpful if you take a close look at the board makeup at an early date. Century, for example, discussed this issue at the board level almost five years before the affiliation. In view of the issues that the industry faces companies should review this matter at the earliest opportunity.

In the affiliation, the board integration went smoothly and set a good example for the rest of the organization. Some of the desireable considerations that are helpful in setting the stage for board integration are listed below.

a. Board members should bring professional expertise that provides balance and a special discipline to the board.
b. Fees paid should be fair and competitive but a very minor part of members' total income.
c. Board members should be independent and in no way beholden to the CEO.
d. The CEO should be responsible to keep the board members interested in the organization by discussing timely industry matters that are relevant to the long-term interests of the company.
e. The leadership within the board should have experienced first hand some of the traumatic changes the company is embarking on and therefore be able to be supportive partners to the CEO who is acting as the change agent for the company.
f. An open and honest environment should be readily apparent at all times in the board in order to build a strong trust relationship with company management.

Techniques that helped specifically in the affiliation:

a. Joint meetings were held with the entire boards from both companies during the affiliation process.
b. Frequent meetings were held with ad hoc committees of the board both independently and jointly and reports made to the entire board at every meeting.
c. Each CEO reported periodically to the other company's board in order to permit board members to ask questions about the affiliation.
d. Outside experts were retained to look over the process on behalf of the board as the affiliation evolved.

As indicated, Century had started looking at the Board makeup and numbers almost five years before the affiliation. Because they were up to speed on industry problems they began to reduce the numbers on the board as retirements occurred in order to keep their options open as they moved into an uncertain future. Consolidations will, by all forecasts, occur and company managements would be well advised to focus on this issue at an early date.

Lesson Nineteen: Do Not Depend Exclusively on Economies of Scale to Ensure Your Future

Do not count exclusively on expense streamlining and economies of scale to achieve optimal value from combining the organizations. Early on, expense reduction may be the primary focus, but revenue side enhancements, that is to say, marketing and sales improvements, are what will ensure that maximum value is obtained from the combination. The affiliation was a unique opportunity in that the primary strategy was to build a sustainable future through the sponsored market but, in addition, it was possible to generate immediate cost savings through economies of scale by combining certain functions. This resulted in the advantage of having the staff witness some immediate benefits by combining the two companies.

The question to consider is whether it would be wise to combine the companies if the only advantage was the economies of scale. Absolutely. In a mature market where all the companies are struggling to hold their share of the market, the "hurdle" rate (the unit cost per item processed) will continue to increase with inflation. There is, of course, a limit to how much expense reduction you can incur without hurting the organization and, therefore, one of the alternatives would be to increase the amount of business processed with the same size staff and information systems support. Combining organizations for the purpose of improving the critical mass and economies of scale will make sense in the near term, but eventually that increasing "hurdle" rate will catch up and it will be necessary to do another combination unless a way has been found to build a sustainable future through the marketing operations.

It should be obvious that whereas the economies of scale achieved through a combination will save money in the near term, expanding the marketing operations will be expensive up-front but will in the long term build the sustainable future that you are trying to achieve.

Lesson Twenty: Integrate the CEO Positions Carefully

Every situation will be unique in this respect. It happened that in the affiliation described here the two CEOs were the same age and close to retirement. Under these circumstances, we suggest that you try to model the joint involvement during the process of the affiliation as you would like the future to unfold after the affiliation is complete.

It might also be advisable to have a contractual agreement as to the mutual retirement date and to precede that with a succession plan. The two CEOs in our story had developed 90 percent of the succession plan before the CEO from Century elected to take normal retirement. The CUNA Mutual CEO announced his intention to retire one year later.

Lesson Twenty-one: Work Hard at Keeping Your Ego in Perspective

It is probably obvious to the reader that many mergers, acquisitions, joint ventures, other forms of combination have failed or fallen short of their objective because of the egos of board members or the CEOs or other individuals within the organizations. While there is not much to be said about this lesson, it needs to be emphasized because it is so critical in the combination process. At times you will believe that the other party is taking advantage of you or that you misread their objectives. What needs to be done is, to the extent humanly possible, set aside your personal agendas and ask yourself who it is you are trying to serve.

Based on the experience of the affiliation the best advice would be to

a. Conduct a role negotiation up front as suggested above.
b. Meet on at least a weekly basis to discuss issues and thus keep all of the problems "on the table."

c. Spend plenty of time listening to the other party and trying to understand each other's perspectives.

d. Keep your focus on the strategic objective and resolve issues in the context of attaining that vision.

Lesson Twenty-two: Maintain Your Spirit of Goodwill

One of the most difficult things to do in times of stress and conflict (and organizational change, no matter how well it is managed, always brings stress and conflict) is to keep in mind that almost everyone is trying to do what he or she thinks is the right thing to do. Understanding this is what we mean by maintaining your spirit of goodwill. It takes a great deal of energy to walk around being upset and angry at others, and this energy is therefore not available to apply to the considerable challenges inherent in accomplishing what is necessary. It is also not much fun. Prior to the affiliation, the Century CEO had often reminded people to "assume good intentions," (AGI) and doing so became labeled as giving each other "AGIs," (pronounced aggies). He continued to urge people to do this during the affiliation. Assuming good intentions on the part of others becomes particularly helpful when trying to avoid the development of "we versus they" thinking that so often attends organizational combinations.

Lesson Twenty-three: Strive to Create a Transparent Organization

In this, our final lesson, we want to describe some ways in which organizations can be prepared for the kind of momentous change involved in combining. We believe that organizations in which there is an emphasis on performance and open, direct communication about that performance (transparent organizations) are more likely to be so prepared. Both of the companies we have been talking about in this book made significant changes to accomplish the affiliation, but Century, being the smaller company and the individual insurance provider, had to make the most revolutionary changes. It had been a small, parochial company recognized for its low-cost products, but it was operating without a market niche. The Century CEO believed that, in the final analysis, his responsibility boiled down to one accountability: to perpetuate the organization on behalf of the policyholders. To do this in a mature industry which was struggling and which had not experienced significant growth in total, he felt he needed to be a catalyst for change for the company to build a sustainable future. He set out to do so in the early 1980s.

At that time, the Hay Company, a management consulting firm active in the insurance industry, was trying to build an instrument that would measure the extent to which a company had managed to build a "climate for performance." They asked the CEOs of eleven companies to participate in developing the instrument. Century joined the project and when it was completed, the CEO went to Philadelphia (Hay's headquarters) to determine what changes needed to be made in his company to create such a climate. He learned a great deal that he was able to use, and the Hay people told him that he was the only one of the eleven CEOs who had followed up on the study. He believed that it was important that he avoid becoming over-involved in putting out the daily fires in his company so that he could maintain his focus on long-term issues. He set about creating an organizational culture characterized by an emphasis on performance and open, direct communication about that performance which he thought of as a "transparent" organization. The principles on which such an organizational culture can be built are described below.

Development of Staff. To perpetuate an organization, one must develop staff that can carry on the task. The Century CEO made it a practice to write detailed appraisals of all of the individuals reporting to him and to have those people prepare extensive self-assessments as well. He then devoted one-half to a full day to conducting each of those reviews. In each case, a development plan was prepared and agreed to by both parties. Reviews were done on an "as needed" basis, but never less than once a year. Frequent discussions, which he called "contextual reviews," were also held. He had some of his appraisals reviewed by an industrial psychologist who knew the people involved and even had the psychologist sit in on some of the reviews to critique the CEO on the clarity of his feedback to his people.

Intense Focus. For significant change to occur, the CEO must give undivided attention to the organization. The Century CEO refused all board invitations except for those from charitable organizations. In addition, he refused to make any investments other than in his own company to avoid any potential conflicts of interest. He desired to convey the point to his people that their future was his agenda.

Board Relationships. A partnership relationship, not an adversarial one, must be developed between the CEO and the board. The CEO of Century insisted that the board have an executive session at which he was not present after every board meeting. The purpose of these meetings was to discuss openly any issues the directors may have had and then to share those issues with the CEO after the meeting. He believed that to maintain focus on long-term objectives, all issues, including any regarding the performance of the CEO, needed to be on the table. New board memberships were decided by the current board members and not by the CEO. In addition, all board members other than the CEO were from outside the organization including the board chairman and the meeting agendas were set by the board chairman in collaboration with the CEO.

Keeping the Board Informed. The board, if they are to be partners in the organization's growth process, must be well informed. Century staff often made presentations to the board so that the board could remain apprised of the staff's development in addition to staying informed on issues. For over ten years prior to the affiliation, Century Board meetings regularly included an agenda item called "organizational renewal." This item was dealt with by the CEO in executive session with the board and it included any concerns the CEO had about the company's future, including staffing issues, strategic concerns, and so forth. This agenda item was used to help the board learn about developments in the industry of concern to the CEO and, later, to discuss the potential of the affiliation with CUNA Mutual. It gave the CEO the opportunity to involve and educate his board "partners" without unnecessarily raising the anxiety of his staff.

Climate for Performance Measures. Century management conducted an internal assessment of their culture and, through a series of discussions, clarified an understanding of the culture they wanted to create. At least every two years, a climate for performance survey, an attitude survey or a management audit was conducted. The intent was to focus continually on improving performance and to measure the progress made. Periodically, an intense focus on a particular function was conducted which Century called a "physical." The purpose was to consider what the function should look like ten years into the future and to decide what changes are needed to reach that objective. Progress was monitored continually, and results shared with the board.

Delegation. The CEO continually reviewed the allocation of his time and activities. The question always was "Is there someone in the organization who could do this more efficiently than I am doing it?" If the answer was yes, he sought to delegate the activity. He tried to keep his focus on the future, and he maintained a highly competent assistant to take care of the details of all of his activities.

Communications. It is important that the staff be regularly updated on progress toward corporate objectives and that they feel a part of the process of achieving those objectives. At Century, regular quarterly communications sessions were held with all employees. Various staff members participated as presenters in these sessions. The CEO was often a participant. He held practice sessions with individuals from different levels in the organization so they could tell him what they had heard him say. This feedback helped him improve the clarity of his presentations.

Self-appraisal. Periodically, the CEO asked his direct reports for feedback on his performance. In addition, he held periodic reviews with his senior managers to discuss the subject, "How are we managing the organization and how do we want to manage it?" These sessions served as checks on his own and the organization's performance. Later on, the senior management conducted a series of open, group appraisals in which they discussed each other's performance in a group and searched for ways in which they could help each other develop.

Asking Others for Input. The Century CEO regularly sought opinions from others, both outside and inside his organization. Within the organization, he employed the following system for decision making. Decisions were referred to as "ones, twos or threes." A "one" was a decision which the CEO was going to make on his own and about which he would simply inform the staff. (There were not many of these.) A "two" was a decision which the CEO was going to make, but on which he was "influencable" and on which he therefore actively sought the staff's input. (There were many such decisions.) A "three" was a decision which the CEO felt should be made by the staff and on which he was willing to go with the majority opinion. (There were also many of these.) The culture of Century was such that people felt comfortable (if the CEO forgot to tell them beforehand) in asking, "Is this a one, a two or a three?"

Building Trust. The CEO had a sign in his office which simply said, "build." To some visitors that sign did not carry any clear message, but it was intended to be a constant reminder that the focus of management must remain on the building of trust within the organization by keeping it "transparent." Century evolved a short list of statements to describe that environment:

1. Trust is earned by treating others with dignity and respect.

2. Success depends on developing the capabilities of all of our associates.
3. Our associates have the creative capacity to solve the organization's problems.
4. Communications must be open, honest, and timely.
5. Performance must be measured by long-term results.

The benefits of building the type of environment suggested above are enormous. Doing so allows the organization's members to devote their resources to accomplishing their vision of the future, to be creative, to be energized and to think in terms of how to reach that vision. It also strengthens people's faith that they can accomplish what they are about because they believe in the organization's purpose, they believe they are supported in their collective effort.

CONCLUSION

As of April 1995, over eight years have passed since the CEOs of CUNA Mutual and Century Companies first met at the seminar at Harvard University. The vast majority of the integration of their organizations has been accomplished, and this book is the story of how it has been done, as well as what has been learned in the process.

During those eight years the consolidation of the financial services industry has continued to take place and, in fact, the pace of that consolidation has increased. It is evident that many more organizational combinations will take place both within and outside of the financial services industry. In that process, the lives of those involved will be permanently affected, just as the lives of the people of CUNA Mutual and Century have been. Many in these two companies have given a great deal of themselves to achieve the successful combination of their organizations. We hope that the telling of their story will afford them the opportunity to reflect positively on what they have accomplished and, at the same time, to give one more gift—the benefit of their experience to help others who will one day travel a similar path.

REFERENCES

Hammer, M., and Champy, J. 1993. *Reengineering the corporation*. New York: Harper.

Mirvis, P., and Marks, M. 1992a. *Managing the merger: Making it Work*. Englewood Cliffs, NJ: Prentice-Hall.

Mirvis, P., and Marks, M. 1992b. The human side of merger planning; assessing and analyzing "fit." *Human Resource Planning* 15, 17–25.

Pritchett, P. 1985. *After the merger: Managing the shockwaves*. Homewood, Ill: Dow Jones-Irwin.

Tichey, N., and Sherman, S. 1993. *Control your destiny or someone else will*. New York: Doubleday.

Index

About the Authors

DAVID A. WHITSETT is Professor of Psychology at the University of Northern Iowa. His previous books include *From Management Theory to Business Sense* and *Scenarios of Change* (Praeger, 1989).

IRVING R. BURLING is the recently retired President and Chief Executive Officer of Century Companies of America.